GRAPH ALGEBRA

**Mathematical Modeling
With a Systems Approach**

Courtney Brown

Series: Quantitative Applications
in the Social Sciences

151

Ⓢ SAGE Publications

Series: Quantitative Applications in the Social Sciences

Series Editor: Tim F. Liao, *Sociology, University of Illinois*
Series Founding Editor: Michael S. Lewis-Beck, *Political Science, University of Iowa*

Editorial Consultants

Richard A. Berk, *Sociology, University of California, Los Angeles*
William D. Berry, *Political Science, Florida State University*
Kenneth A. Bollen, *Sociology, University of North Carolina, Chapel Hill*
Linda B. Bourque, *Public Health, University of California, Los Angeles*
Jacques A. Hagenaars, *Social Sciences, Tilburg University*
Sally Jackson, *Communications, University of Arizona*
Richard M. Jaeger (recently deceased), *Education, University of North Carolina, Greensboro*
Gary King, *Department of Government, Harvard University*
Roger E. Kirk, *Psychology, Baylor University*
Helena Chmura Kraemer, *Psychiatry and Behavioral Sciences, Stanford University*
Peter Marsden, *Sociology, Harvard University*
Helmut Norpoth, *Political Science, SUNY, Stony Brook*
Frank L. Schmidt, *Management and Organization, University of Iowa*
Herbert Weisberg, *Political Science, The Ohio State University*

Publisher

Sara Miller McCune, SAGE Publications, Inc.

Quantitative Applications in the Social Sciences

A SAGE PUBLICATIONS SERIES

Quantitative Applications in the Social Sciences

A SAGE PUBLICATIONS SERIES

Series/Number 07–151

GRAPH ALGEBRA

Mathematical Modeling
With a Systems Approach

Courtney Brown
Emory University

SAGE Publications
Los Angeles • London • New Delhi • Singapore

University of
Wisconsin-Madison
Libraries

For information:

Sage Publications, Inc.
2455 Teller Road
Thousand Oaks, California 91320
E-mail: order@sagepub.com

Sage Publications India Pvt. Ltd.
B 1/I 1 Mohan Cooperative Industrial Area
Mathura Road, New Delhi 110 044
India

Sage Publications Ltd.
1 Oliver's Yard
55 City Road
London EC1Y 1SP
United Kingdom

Sage Publications Asia-Pacific Pte. Ltd.
33 Pekin Street #02-01
Far East Square
Singapore 048763

Printed in the United States of America

Library of Congress Cataloging-in-Publication Data

Brown, Courtney, 1952–
Graph algebra: Mathematical modeling with a systems approach / Courtney Brown.
    p. cm. — (Quantitative applications in the social sciences; 151)
Includes bibliographical references and index.
ISBN 978-1-4129-4109-9 (pbk.)
    1. Social sciences—Mathematical models. 2. Graph theory. I. Title.
H61.25.B76 2008
300.1'5115—dc22

                    2007004811

This book is printed on acid-free paper.

07   08   09   10   11   10   9   8   7   6   5   4   3   2   1

Acquisitions Editors:	Lisa Cuevas Shaw and Vicki Knight
Associate Editor:	Sean Connelly
Production Editor:	Melanie Birdsall
Copy Editor:	QuADS Prepress (P) Ltd.
Typesetter:	C&M Digitals (P) Ltd.
Proofreader:	Kevin Gleason
Indexer:	Sheila Bodell
Cover Designer:	Candice Harman
Marketing Manager:	Stephanie Adams

CONTENTS

SERIES EDITOR'S INTRODUCTION

Together with Brown's *Differential Equations: A Modeling Approach,* the current book on graph algebra provides a nice extension to mathematical applications in the social sciences, a topic covered by not so many volumes in our series (e.g., Nos. 108 and 109 on basic math for social scientists, No. 110 on calculus as the focus, and No. 27 on difference equations as a method for dynamic modeling). Mathematical applications can be part and parcel of quantitative applications in social scientific research though they have so far been overshadowed by statistical ones.

Whereas the method of graph algebra has been around for over three decades in the social sciences, the publication of Brown's *Graph Algebra: Mathematical Modeling With a Systems Approach* (as well as his earlier book on differential equations) is timely because there has been a resurgence of interest in the linkage between social theories and empirical models via closer formal correspondence. In recent years, the National Science Foundation funded a series of summer institutes on the topic of the Empirical Implications of Theoretical Models (EITM), hosted by some top research universities: EITM I in 2002 at Harvard, EITM II in 2003 at Michigan, EITM III in 2004 at Duke, EITM IV in 2005 at UC, Berkeley, and EITM V in 2006 at Michigan.

The themes of the EITM summer institutes have been fairly consistent. In 2006, for example, the particular foci were institutions and institutional analysis; empirical evaluation of causality; and complexity: diversity, networks, adaptation, and emergence. In 2005, the areas concentrated on were models of political institutions, bargaining and coercion models, and coordination games. Institutional analysis can serve as a case in point. Some of the prominent issues in institutional models include the analysis of equilibrium, the formation of collective actions, coalition governance, and bargaining dynamics. All these are theoretical issues that can be studied with the assistance of graph algebra, which can provide a formal representation of how such theory may work empirically.

In a nutshell, both *Graph Algebra* and *Differential Equations* offer an approach to a better understanding as well as a better representation of social and political theory by using mathematical models that are isomorphic to the theory, both linear and nonlinear, and in both discrete and continuous time. The current book too gives a good example of connecting methods more typically used in the engineering and physical sciences to the social sciences.

This is not to say that statistical methods cannot be used for the understanding of empirical implications of theoretical models; they can. However, mathematical models can be formed with a much closer linkage to theory, and in that respect, Brown's book on graph algebra gives social scientists another valuable guide for a proper understanding of political, psychological, and social behavior.

—Tim F. Liao
Series Editor

ACKNOWLEDGMENTS

This book is dedicated to Fernando Cortés, Adam Przeworski, and John Sprague, the original developers of the graph algebra language. It has been nearly 30 years since I was first introduced to the subject of graph algebra by John Sprague at Washington University. This occurred in the second of a two-semester graduate-level course on mathematical modeling, and words cannot do justice in describing the nearly visceral level of excitement that was felt at the time by all the students as we listened to those lectures. We had long been exposed to mathematical modeling, but what always seemed a mystery was how social scientists could come up the algebraic specification of great models in the first place. This was especially true of nonlinear models. We understood the linear regression model thoroughly, and we hungered to find a way to move beyond it, or perhaps, to escape from it. We found such a liberating path in the language of graph algebra. I thank John for introducing me to this language, and for approaching the subject with the type of excitement that only comes with a feeling of new discovery. I also want to thank Hank Heitowit at the University of Michigan who invited me for 12 years to teach graph algebra at the ICPSR Summer Program. Finally, the series editor, Tim Futing Liao, helped shepherd this manuscript with sensitivity and care, and the anonymous reviewers gave exceptionally useful advice, for all of which I am deeply grateful. I also thank Rafal Raciborski for carefully reading an early version of the manuscript and for offering thoughtful advice.

Sage Publications gratefully acknowledges the contributions of reviewers Eric Plutzer, Pennsylvania State University, and Gudmund Iversen, Swarthmore College.

GRAPH ALGEBRA

Mathematical Modeling
With a Systems Approach

Courtney Brown
Emory University

1. SYSTEMS ANALYSIS

Rarely has a new approach to theory development offered as great a potential for impacting the way social scientists develop mathematical models of social and political phenomena as is the case with graph algebra. Graph algebra is both a tool and a language that originates from systems theory. It was originally developed by three social scientists, Fernando Cortés, Adam Przeworski, and John Sprague, in a seminal volume *(Systems Analysis for Social Scientists)* that first appeared in 1974. In this book, I both explain and extend the language of graph algebra, as well as update its application to address contemporary mathematical and social-theoretical themes. Thus, this book is not merely a reference work of ideas previously presented elsewhere; there also is a great deal of entirely new material in these pages. This reflects the fact that graph algebra—like any living language—continues to grow as the theoretical needs of social scientists expand and evolve. That graph algebra continues to speak to the needs of social and political theorists is a testament to the power of the ideas of its three originators.

In its essence, the use of graph algebra assists social scientists in developing new and surprisingly sophisticated mathematical models of complex social phenomena. This is true for both linear and nonlinear models. Social scientists use the graph algebra language to translate social scientific theories into mathematical formulas or models. Indeed, a creative thinker can often use graph algebra to algebraically "flesh out" even the most complicated and sophisticated of theories. Importantly, graph algebra can empower social scientists to "escape" from a dependence on simple linear regression models that are based on rudimentary intercepts and slopes that reveal little more than correlations within a set of variables. Moreover, regression can often be creatively applied to fully estimate intellectually appealing graph algebra models using commonly available statistical software. This allows social

1

scientists to incorporate greater theoretical depth in the algebra of their models while still utilizing known statistical procedures.

Some readers will find this book to be highly correspondent with recent initiatives in theory building in the social sciences, perhaps best typified by efforts pursued by the National Science Foundation. Not long ago, the National Science Foundation launched an initiative called "The Empirical Implications of Theoretical Models" (EITM). The EITM (2002) report from the National Science Foundation states,

> A schism has developed between those who engage in formal modeling that is highly mathematical, and those who employ empirical modeling which emphasizes applied statistics. As a consequence, a good deal of research in political science is competent in one technical area, but lacking in another, that is, a formal approach with substandard (or no) empirical tests or an empirical approach without formal clarity. Such impaired competency contributes to a failure to identify the proximate causes explicated in a theory and, in turn, increases the difficulty of achieving a meaningful increase in scientific knowledge. (p. 1)

While this book is aimed at all the social sciences (and thus is by no means limited to the discipline of political science), the observation that efforts are needed in many areas to better link social and political theories to testable empirical models is worth noting. The question is, "How does one do this?" And even more pointedly, "How does one teach someone to do this?" Coming up with an intellectually interesting algebraic specification has historically been one of the most challenging things most researchers have ever had to do, which is why so many scientists rely on the "canned" linear regression model. Some scholars, after noting the difficultly and seriousness of the problem, have argued that researchers can either search for their own model specification based on their own theory or, failing that, perhaps use statistical methods that impose no structure on the analysis. This latter approach would use "theory-less methods" (see, e.g., Signorino & Yilmaz, 2003). What this book offers is a means by which such linkages can be made using a highly practical new graphical language that empowers social scientists to develop nuanced algebraic models of their theories that contain a level of intellectual sophistication that might have previously appeared forbidding, or perhaps even impossible.

There are a number of highly prominent examples of the use of graph algebra in the social sciences. Sometimes graph algebra is used in the theory-building stage of a project to assist in the development of a model's algebra for a social or political process, but the graph algebra itself is not presented in the final printed report. This is the case with the seminal volume *Paper Stones: A History of Electoral Socialism* by Przeworski and

Sprague (1986), which contains a theoretically rich analysis of the development of leftist voting in Europe during much of the 20th century. In this case, while graph algebra was used early in the research to develop a sophisticated model of leftist voting, the book itself presents (and explains) only the normal algebraic version of the model.

In other cases, the graph algebra itself is presented in the final report of a research project as a means of helping to simplify the presentation of a complex model that might otherwise appear inhibiting for some readers. This indeed is the case with research by Duvall and Freeman (1983), in which they develop and analyze a model that helps explain how certain elites dominate the industrialization processes in many developing nations. This is also the case in some of my own research in which I present a model of congressional voting in the United States using graph algebra to help readers retain a wide-angle view of a somewhat complicated political theory (Brown, 1991, see especially the appendix to Chapter 7). In other cases, graph algebra has been effectively included in a final report as a means of emphasizing the linkage between the model and the social or political theory. This is often useful even in situations in which the normal algebra itself is not so intimidating, as in the case of an analysis of electoral institutionalization and voter mobilization in many European nations by Przeworski (1975). Thus, graph algebra can be used "behind the scenes" to develop a sophisticated algebraic specification of a complex theory, or it can be used in a more up-front manner that also assists with the presentation of the theory itself. Either way, researchers can use graph algebra to help develop, analyze, and present social and political theories that incorporate surprising levels of intellectual richness.

Before describing the details of graph algebra, it is worth placing it in the context of systems theory. Why approach mathematical modeling from the perspective of systems analysis? Many scientists—whether they work in the social sciences, physical sciences, natural sciences, or engineering— often think in terms of systems. Just about everything influences something else, which in turn either feeds back into itself or affects something different. Consider human organizations. We live in systems. Our nations, towns, international associations, friendship networks, and families are systems. We have court systems, electoral systems, presidential systems, parliamentary systems, and bureaucratic systems. Our small groups and associations are systems, just as an inner-city gang is a system regulated by norms that are enforced with punishments and rewards that maintain membership, identity, and coherence. The list of systems that surround us goes on and on, seemingly without end.

Our biology is organized in terms of systems. Our bodies are living systems, as are each of the smaller components of our bodies, such as our cells, our nervous systems, our immune systems, our digestive systems, and our reproductive systems. Each system depends on another system for its functioning and/or survival, with each level adding new complexity to the macro-organization of higher levels of systems. The ecology of a lake is a system of species, with each species having a direct or indirect influence on the others. A wolf den is a system with a clear sense of hierarchical dominance. An ant colony is a system with a highly differentiated work hierarchy.

Our physical environment is organized in terms of systems. Houses are filled with systems. The regulation and control of water in our toilets functions as a system. We live in temperature-regulated environments, with heating and air conditioning apparatuses that are controlled as a system. Even a toaster oven is a self-regulating system.

The smallest and largest parts of our universe are organized as systems. Atoms are systems that we identify by name in the periodic table. Entangled photons are quantum systems. Galaxies are systems, as are nebulae that give birth to new stars. Our own solar system is a system that both inspires us and helps us to measure time and track the seasons.

We organize our thoughts systematically, in the sense that we arrange different thoughts such that they complete a pattern that is itself an identifiable conceptual entity. Indeed, the way in which we process our thoughts is a system that responds to inputs (stimuli, new information, etc.) and produces outputs (physical movement, decisions, etc.). It is natural for us to think in terms of systems because we are enmeshed in them at every level of our existence. For this reason, it is inevitable that we would seek to use a language that helps us describe our systems in a manner that lends itself well to analysis. This need gives rise to "systems analysis."

The term *systems theory* means different things to different people. Early pioneers in the field now known as *general systems theory* include Ludwig von Bertalanffy (1976), W. Ross Ashby (1956), and Gerald M. Weinberg (1975). By most estimates, the large and diverse general systems literature dates back to the 1940s, although the precursors to general systems theory predate even that. James Grier Miller (1978) made a major contribution in expanding the definition and scope of *general living systems theory,* a more specialized approach to general systems theory as it applies to living organisms of all types. On the other hand, electrical engineers look at systems theory from the perspective of the flow of electrons through circuitry. Other engineers see systems theory from the perspective of mechanical inputs and outputs. Computer programmers look at systems theory from the perspective of code that specifies a sequential set of instructions. Still others think of systems theory in other ways.

The focus of this book is on a specific set of mathematical tools that arise mostly from systems theory as it is encountered in both electrical and physical engineering. But we address social systems here, not engineering systems, regardless of where the mathematical techniques came from originally. Also, no effort is spent trying to systematically integrate the material presented here with the general systems literature. Indeed, there is only a tangential link between the contents of this book and the way systems theory is applied in fields outside of the social sciences. The only substantial connection of these other approaches to systems theory is the consistent theme that one can investigate a system by understanding how its internal parts are arranged and how they operate in a coordinated manner.

Systems theory as described in this book dates back to the seminal book by Cortés et al. (1974). In that volume, the authors translated and reinterpreted mathematical methods that are predominantly described in the engineering literature such that these methods could be productively used by social scientists. While their efforts were successful from a utilitarian point of view, there are nonetheless considerable superficial differences in the way social systems are described using their approach when compared with styles common to the engineering disciplines. Most notably, Cortés et al. describe systems using "graph algebra," which engineers will more commonly reference as "block diagrams." Also, engineers tend to favor "signal-flow graphs" rather than block diagrams since they are more compact. However, the compactness of signal-flow graphs leaves them both more terse and abstract than would be helpful to most social scientists. Outside of the engineering literature, block diagrams are also quite commonly used to describe more general and nonmathematical process-related ideas connected to general systems theory, and this intellectual baggage would only serve to confuse a new application of systems mathematics as it applies to the social sciences. Thus, Cortés et al. chose to mix the block-diagram approach with the algebraic utility of signal-flow graphs, which led to the term *graph algebra* to identify a mathematical style of representing systems that was uniquely tailored to describing social scientific phenomena.

Graph algebra is best described as a language for translating social scientific theories into mathematical formulas. The language is designed to ease the model-building process such that users of graph algebra can develop more sophisticated models of complex social scientific ideas than might otherwise be possible. We currently do not know the limits of how broadly graph algebra can be applied to social scientific questions as it is still quite commonplace for researchers to propose and develop new uses and innovative applications of the language. For example, there have been significant advances in the mathematics of dynamical systems since graph algebra was first invented. This is particularly true with respect to systems of differential and difference equations, chaos theory, and catastrophe theory. Thus, this book both describes and extends the language of graph algebra, as well as updates its use with respect to some of these new applications.

Structure and Function

At the core of systems theory is the identification and description of a system's structure, its function, and the response of the system to inputs. In the most basic terms, a system's structure is the collection and arrangement of its parts. The system's structure is essentially unchanging. Some social scientists may object to the notion that anything in human affairs is static, and I have no fundamental quarrel with this position. However, there are many things that remain approximately the same for a long period of time, and for our purposes this is sufficient for us to proceed with the description of social systems. For example, it is true that all democracies evolve, and with that evolution comes change. But the electoral systems of most democracies persist unchanged in their essential characteristics for years, and often decades. Change can occur when, say, in the United States the voting franchise was extended to women in 1920, when African Americans were able to vote in large numbers with the banishment of the Jim Crow laws in the 1960s, or when the voting franchise was extended to 18- to 20-year-olds in the 1970s. But between those years, and again after the 1970s, the electoral system in the United States has changed very little in terms of its structure. Moreover, if we reconceptualize vote mobilization as an input into an electoral system rather than as a part of the structure of the system, we can argue that only the mobilization inputs have changed and that the voting system itself has changed very little since the American Civil War.

We do not directly observe the structure of a system in the manner in which we observe, say, an apple. The structure is only a theoretical concept. It says that certain rules are followed that organize human activity. For example, the division of the American electoral system into separate states and congressional districts is part of the structure of the system. The fact that a concomitant presidential election every 4 years boosts voting turnout in every other congressional election (which occurs in a 2-year cycle) is a feature of the structure of the American electoral system. The use of a winner-take-all ballot and the consequent promotion of a two-party system is part of the structure of the system. In a parliamentary system of government, proportional representation is part of the structure of the system. In governments that have hybrid forms of democratic representation, presidents, prime ministers, district-based parliamentary seats, and party lists are all parts of the structure of an electoral system.

Consider some of the many rules that surround us as members of any society. These rules are elements of larger structures that we can identify as the infrastructure that both creates and supports our social systems. For example, in most societies there are rules against marrying close relatives.

Stock market trading prohibits insider disclosures of company information. The Federal Reserve Board in the United States meets in private and often delays the reporting of its deliberations to avoid volatile market reactions. The trading of endangered species is prohibited. Gases that destroy the ozone layer in our atmosphere are often restricted in their use. The safety of the workplace is often regulated in developed countries. Zoning restricts the use of private property. Price controls place restrictions on the natural interplay between demand and supply. All these examples are parts of structures for complex systems within which we live. We do not physically see these structures, but we know the rules that define them. When we talk about "social theory," we are really discussing the identification and analysis of social structures. We investigate social structures to understand why they produce the social reality that we actually do observe.

All system structures provide a function. The function of a system is what the structure does. In elementary systems, the function of a system transforms the inputs into outputs via a forward path. That is, a system's structure receives an input, and that input is changed in some way to produce an output. In slightly more advanced systems, there can be a feedback path in which the output reenters the system as a new input. This is how feedback works in the case of a microphone that picks up sound from speakers and then feeds that sound back into the amplifier, which then sends it back out to the speakers, and on it goes until a loud squeal is produced by the speakers. In that case, the structure of the system is the microphone, the amplifier, and the speakers, all of which are connected in a certain order. The function of the system is the transforming of input sounds registered by the microphone into output sounds produced by the speakers. In the absence of feedback, the amplifier is the only element of the forward path that connects the microphone to the speakers.

Thus, a system's structure transforms inputs into outputs via its function. The inputs vary, and the outputs vary. Intermediate states of the system that exist after the inputs have gone into the system but before the outputs are in their final form also vary. But the structure of the system is fixed, or invariant. This means that the rules that define the structure of the system remain static for a sufficiently long period of time to allow us to investigate the system's functioning.

Thus, when we speak of systems, we are normally examining synchronic change. This is change as found in the inputs and outputs, but within the context of a system's structure that is invariant. When the system's structure changes, then we have diachronic change. Diachronic change normally means that a new system has taken over and that the old system is obsolete. In practical terms, diachronic change typically requires social scientists to develop a new theory, and a new model. However, it is worth pointing out at this juncture that systems can sometimes be sufficiently sophisticated in their structure such that what once may have been considered an emergence of diachronic change can be explained within the context of a single model's experience of synchronic change. For example, this is a prominent feature of models that employ catastrophe theory (see Brown, 1995b).

An Overview of the Substantive
Examples Found in Subsequent Chapters

The greatest strength of graph algebra is its flexibility—as a language—in working within a great variety of substantive contexts. For this reason, I have attempted to show throughout this book how graph algebra works using a diverse collection of examples. Some of these examples are very basic, as would be needed heuristically to convey the essential mechanics of the graph algebra grammar. But other examples are much more extensive, raising new and potentially provocative specification questions regarding well-known models that have existed in the extant social science literatures for some time.

In Chapter 2, I begin by using graph algebra to "re-create" the linear regression model. This is an especially useful example because it allows the later (and more complex) models to be placed in stark contrast with the nearly overbearing simplicity of the linear model. I then develop a simple voter mobilization model that applies some of the basic feedback capabilities of graph algebra and finish the chapter by using graph algebra to develop the well-known Keynesian multiplier from economics.

Chapter 3 further extends the voter mobilization model as I introduce the use of time operators with graph algebra, especially in systems involving feedback and control. In one case, I discuss this with respect to the elections held in Iraq in 2005. But I also discuss how these ideas can be related to other substantive areas, such as population growth in China. At the end of Chapter 3, I show one approach to estimating graph algebra models using an example of labor union membership in the United States.

Chapters 4 and 5 describe how graph algebra can be used with systems of equations. In both these chapters, I develop an extensive and running example of the arms race model of Lewis Fry Richardson. I first show how Richardson's original model can be specified using graph algebra and then I demonstrate how his model may in fact be a reduced-form version of a number of more complicated models. The more complicated models often seem to capture the substantive intent of Richardson's ideas more than his original specification, and these examples are used to demonstrate how easy it is to work theoretically with graph algebra. I also demonstrate one approach to estimating these models using ordinary least squares. While Chapter 4 focuses on the setting of discrete time, Chapter 5 moves the discussion to continuous time models.

Chapter 6 introduces the rich topic (and one of my personal favorites) of how to use graph algebra to work with nonlinear systems. While there are a great many algebraic approaches to nonlinearity, I organize the discussion beginning with relatively simple mechanics involving nonlinear filters before turning to more complex forms. As the chapter progresses, I explain how graph algebra can be used to model various versions of logistic growth, a common feature of many population models. I also address how graph algebra can be applied relatedly to the ideas of concurrent and lagged environmental decay, global warming, and rising sea levels. The chapter then turns to the issue of chaos, and graph algebra is used to specify the equations that produce Lorenz's well-known chaotic strange attractor. Finally, I return to Richardson's arms race model by showing how one can explore this model in combination with a forced oscillator.

Chapter 7 introduces the idea of using conditional paths with graph algebra. I begin by describing how conditional paths relate to important theory-building ideas that are current in the sociological literatures. I then show how graph algebra can work with decision or choice theory. It is possible to use choice theory to manipulate the structure of a system as it is operating in real time. Applications include a revised look at Richardson's arms race model, as well as how to model the transition from authoritarian to democratic rule in China using catastrophe theory. These ideas allow theorists to blend the two worlds of individual choice and stimulus-response that so often (and perhaps unnecessarily) seem at polar opposites of the theoretical spectrum.

In Chapter 8, I show how shocks and other forms of stochasticity can be introduced into a graph algebraic representation of a system. Here, I return to the logistic model and offer an example of how this model may be modified using graph algebra to address the issue of population growth in the context of an environmental disaster. I then extend this discussion to a similar context, but with respect to a rapid rise in oil prices. Both these issues are highly topical in contemporary times, and researchers will want to use graph algebra to add realistic complexity to their models of these and other vitally important topics.

Chapter 9 turns to the issue of the implied theoretical content of the graph algebra language itself. Here, I categorize three types of system equilibria, system stability, variable stability, and meta-equilibrium, within a system cascade. Here is also where I approach the subject of graph algebra using the broadest theoretical brush, and I relate the issue of system stability to ideas of societal development raised by theorists such as Nisbet, Rostow, Organski, Ingelhart, and Pye. Graph algebra need not be limited to those realms in which one wants to resolve a parameter's value. Indeed, graph algebra can be used narrowly to specify a model for a specific question or problem or broadly to theorize within intellectual realms of significant expanse, or anywhere in between.

2. GRAPH ALGEBRA BASICS

The use of graph algebra can yield marked benefits to theory building in the social sciences, and it is useful to view these benefits when considering the linear regression model. Arguably, the most common model used in the social sciences is the linear regression model. While many approaches to parameter estimation exist for linear models, the ultimate result is typically a table with a list of independent variables and their associated parameter estimates and standard errors. From this perspective, the list of variables in the table *is* the model. Specification concerns usually revolve around the question of whether or not a researcher has omitted one or more important variables from the analysis, although sometimes the issue of functional form also is involved.

While graph algebra does not reduce a researcher's need to be aware of potential omitted variable specification problems, it does allow the researcher much greater flexibility with respect to designing innovative and intellectually appealing functional forms. As an absolute minimum, graph algebra allows us to develop more sophisticated model specifications such that the algebraic form of the model becomes as important as the variables that exist within that form. Thus, systems theory as it is expressed through graph algebra offers a means of developing algebraic formulations that correspond with social and political theories that are more complex and sophisticated than the ubiquitous linear form. Thus, as a movement away from the linear model, the use of graph algebra encourages the development of increasingly interesting scientific theories. Moreover, as will become clear by the end of this book, such theories find their origin in the thinking of the theorist, not in the graph algebra itself.

A researcher gains the benefits of graph algebra by mastering its functionality as a language. Graph algebra is the language that we use to describe a system's structure and functioning. With graph algebra we identify the parts of the system's structure, and then we connect those parts in a process that identifies the structure's functioning. Thus, the system's structure leads to an understanding of its functioning. Once we have identified a system's structure and functioning using graph algebra, we then turn to an analysis of the response of the system with respect to variations in inputs. Ultimately, we use graph algebra to describe a social process and to identify causal inference with a system's perspective. Most graph algebra models can be fully estimated with respect to a body of data, and researchers will in general want to do this. However, one can also use graph algebra to develop models that are used only analytically. Subsequent analysis of the model (estimated or otherwise) can take many forms, including prediction or forecasting, various analytics, and simulation.

In terms of mechanics, graph algebra uses elements to transform inputs into outputs. The elements are the parts of the system's structure that go between the inputs and the outputs. The elements contain operators that describe how those elements work to transform one state of the system into another state of the system. One can think of a "state of the system" as a measuring point during the process of transforming inputs into outputs. As inputs are changed into outputs, they experience various intermediate conditions. These intermediate conditions are the states of the system. An element works on a state of the system to transform it into another state of the system. All of this happens before the entire system eventually gives birth to a final output.

In graph algebra, elements are normally represented by boxes. Operators go inside the boxes. The collection of connected elements constitutes the system's structure. Typically, inputs go to the left of this structure, and outputs are placed to the right of this structure.

Inputs, Outputs, and the Forward Path

All systems require inputs and outputs. In many situations often associated with single-equation models, the inputs are typically considered the independent variables of the model, whereas the output is the dependent variable of the model. I write "in many situations" because it is possible for independent variables not to be explicit inputs, such as with the variable *time* in many of the continuous-time dynamic models presented later in this book. Also, sometimes inputs are not really "independent," as in the multiple regression sense of the word. Indeed, the idea that one variable is "independent" and another variable is "dependent" normally implies that the independent variable causes change in the dependent variable and nothing of significant importance is causing change to the independent variable. That is, the causality is one-way only, from independent to dependent. But in many interesting systems, the idea that a variable is truly independent can be a misnomer. Indeed, the essence of systems analysis in the first place is that everything affects everything else, or a least some other things. So it is possible for systems to exist that do not really have any authentically independent variables. For this reason, we normally use the word *input* rather than *independent variable* when talking about systems. But this choice of terminology will vary depending on a particular theoretical context and a researcher's preferences.

There is a similar issue with the use of the words *dependent variable* to describe a system's output. We can use these words so long as we recognize that their use may not be entirely parallel to the way they are used in statistical analyses, such as with multiple regression, since dependency can reside in many places within a system. The more common usage when talking about systems is to call the dependent variable the output. Again, this choice of terminology will depend on the theoretical context and a researcher's preferences. Also, multiple-equation models may have more than one output or dependent variable. More intuitively, the inputs are what go into the system to make it work, and the outputs are the result of the system's processing of the inputs. In mechanical terms, one can think of gasoline as an input, the engine as the system, and forward movement of the car as the output.

It is best to describe graph algebra with a simple heuristic example. Using an example drawn from human behavior, let us say that workers in a political campaign are doing door-to-door canvassing for potential voters to support their candidate. Let us also say that a certain proportion of these interactions result in a successful mobilization of voters. This is a simple system, and for the purpose of keeping this example system simple, so that we can initially focus only on the graph algebra that describes its structure, I am purposely avoiding ideas that might make this system more realistic and thus more complicated. (For example, one might ask if some of those contacted by the campaign workers might have voted regardless of whether or not the workers knocked on their door.) The input to this system is the canvassing activity done by the campaign workers, and the output to this system is the mobilization of voters. This is represented using graph algebra in Figure 2.1.

In Figure 2.1, C_t is the input to the system, and it represents the number of people who are contacted by the campaign workers during the canvassing activity at time t. The box in the figure is an element of the system, and it contains the parameter p. Parameters are one form of operator, and they are called "parameters of proportional transformation" in the language of graph algebra. What this means in terms of the model in Figure 2.1 is that a certain proportion (p) of the people canvassed by the campaign workers [C_t] will become mobilized to vote. The output of the system is V_t, and this

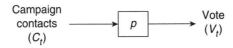

Figure 2.1   A Simple System of Voter Mobilization Using
Graph Algebra

represents the number of people who are mobilized to vote. The path from C_t to V_t is called the "forward path," since the activity of the system moves "forward" from input to output along this path. The convention is that forward paths typically flow from left to right.

Graph algebra always translates into an algebraic statement. In the case of Figure 2.1, the algebraic statement for this graph algebra model is $V_t = pC_t$. This results from the most basic rule of graph algebra:

Graph Algebra Rule #1: *Things that flow along the same path are multiplied.*

Thus, we begin with the input and multiply it by anything that is located along the forward path. We then set that equal to the output of the system. This simple model says that some proportion (p) of the campaign contacts [C_t] is transformed into voters [V_t], which means that we multiply p by C_t to obtain V_t.

It is now easy to use graph algebra to represent a simple linear regression equation of the sort commonly used in many statistical analyses. This will also allow us to introduce the second most basic rule of graph algebra. This linear regression model is presented in Figure 2.2 with a model having four independent variables, an intercept, and one dependent variable. The error term is omitted here for simplicity.

In Figure 2.2, the graph algebra model describes a person's probability of voting as a function of the person's income, level of education, self-described partisan identification, and a contextual measure of the partisan composition of the neighborhood within which he or she lives. Note that there are five forward paths in this figure. Four of the forward paths are a result of the inputs from the four independent variables described above, and I describe the fifth forward path below. The algebraic equation that results from the graph in Figure 2.2 is shown as Equation 2.1:

$$\text{Vote} = \beta_0 + \beta_1(\text{Income}) + \beta_2(\text{Education}) + \beta_3(\text{PID}) + \beta_4(\text{Context}), \quad [2.1]$$

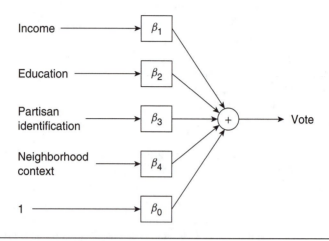

Figure 2.2　　A Simple Regression Model With Four Independent
　　　　　　　　Variables, an Intercept, and One Dependent Variable

where PID stands for partisan identification and context stands for neighborhood context. Note that all the forward paths in Figure 2.2 get added
together in Equation 2.1. This introduces the second most basic rule of
graph algebra:

Graph Algebra Rule #2: *Add paths that merge together at an
intersection.*

Note also that in Figure 2.2 there is an additional forward path that contains
an input of 1 and the parameter β_0. This reflects how many computer pro-
grams calculate an intercept for an estimated regression line, in the sense
that a column of 1s is typically added to a data matrix as a new variable.
Thus, in computational terms, an intercept is actually nothing more than a
slope times the "variable" 1, which in practice simply leaves us with an
additive constant. Finally, note that the model in Figure 2.2 is static, in the
sense that time plays no role in structuring the relationship between these
variables. This is simply a model that specifies how the values of the four
independent variables, which reflect qualities of selected individuals, affect
the value of the dependent variable. In this instance, there is no ambiguity
in using the terms *independent variables* and *dependent variable* instead of
inputs and *output,* respectively, since graph algebra is being used to describe a multiple regression setting in which the former terms are totally
appropriate and the issue of causality is clear. Also, readers should note that
the model is purposely simple, and to keep it useful as a heuristic vehicle to

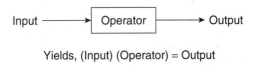

Yields, (Input) (Operator) = Output

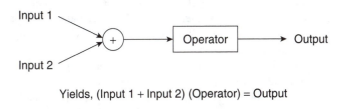

Yields, (Input 1 + Input 2) (Operator) = Output

Figure 2.3   The General Application of Rules #1 and #2 of
                    Graph Algebra

demonstrate the mechanics of graph algebra, other factors that might make it more realistic (and thus more complicated) are avoided.

In general, the application of the first two rules of graph algebra is summarized in Figure 2.3. Note the use of the term *operator* in the element boxes in Figure 2.3. A parameter of proportional transformation is one type of operator that can be used in an element. Other operators are discussed later in this book. Note also that in the example given in the lower part of Figure 2.3 two separate inputs are added together before both of them are "sent" through the same operator on the forward path. These are just heuristic examples of a limitless arrangement of inputs, operators, and outputs. Also, in situations in which there are two inputs, both the inputs do not have to enter the model on the far left. It is possible to enter an input or to place an operator nearly anywhere in graph algebra as long as it all makes sense from a social theory perspective.

Feedback Loops and Mason's Rule

Regulation and control are primary strengths of modeling using graph algebra. Feedback loops are typically used to accomplish regulation and control. A feedback loop is like an input, but its origin is from within the system itself, not from outside of the system. In many systems, the output reenters the system as another input. As mentioned previously, this is exactly what happens with a microphone and speakers when the sound from the speakers feeds back into the microphone, often causing a loud squeal.

Let us return to the earlier example in which campaign workers were canvassing for potential voters. After campaign workers talk to potential voters, some of these people will be mobilized to support the candidate or issue that is discussed. Some of these mobilized people may subsequently begin to talk to their neighbors, friends, and coworkers trying to convince them also to support the cause. Thus, the newly mobilized people are reentering the vote-mobilization system as a new input. They are not the original campaign workers, so they cannot be included as part of that original input. Rather, they are separate. But they too will interact with people just as do the original campaign workers, which means that a proportion of these new interactions will result in additional support for the campaign. This is the same as it was with the original campaign workers.

The general depiction of a feedback loop using graph algebra is shown in Figure 2.4. This figure demonstrates a positive feedback loop, in the sense that the output of the system feeds back into the system as a positive input. The two examples described above, one involving feedback with a microphone and speakers and the other involving campaign interactions, are both instances of positive feedback. But the microphone example is dynamic, in the sense that the squeal from the speakers (and thus the degree of feedback) changes over time. However, note that in Figure 2.4 there is no indication of how time would be involved in the process, since neither the input nor the output is subscripted with t. This kind of system is called a "static system."

Static systems are conceptually different from a "simultaneous system," which is described below, since a static system is independent of time entirely. Linear regression models that relate one dependent variable to a list of independent variables are common examples of static systems as long as none of the variables are subscripted by time. For example, relating income to education via a correlation analysis is a static comparison, as opposed to relating income to education at a particular point in time, which assumes that the relation could be different at a different point in time. This distinction will become more important to us later when we begin using time-based operators with graph algebra.

One might naturally ask how a campaign feedback process can be static (or simultaneous) since it must take place over time. This depends on how we conceptualize the feedback process. Later in this book, time operators are introduced that allow one to specify exactly when the feedback process occurs relative to the other parts of the system. But such time operators do not appear in Figure 2.4. With feedback loops, a fraction of the output reenters the system to eventually show up again as an output, and a fraction of that output reenters the system yet again through the feedback loop . . . and

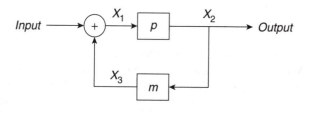

Figure 2.4   A Positive Feedback Loop

on and on it goes. With static systems, the feedback parameter (in this case m) represents the summation of these ongoing feedback cycles, as if the process is in equilibrium, or perhaps at the conclusion of a conceptually bounded time span such as an election campaign.

It is also important to note that when an output reenters the system through a feedback loop, the reentry does not operate as a subtraction from the output (thus diminishing the output). Thus, a feedback process does not remove the output to reuse it. For example, the microphone does not take sound away from the speakers when it reenters some of the output back into the system's amplification process. The output is still the output; it is simply fed back into the system.

Note the variables X_1, X_2, and X_3 in Figure 2.4. These are states of the system, which are values of the system at various points within the system. With graph algebra, one never leaves the states of the system in the final algebra of the model. The states of the system are used only as algebraic conveniences to help us determine the model's final form. For example, in this system we have

$$X_1 = Input + X_3,$$
$$X_2 = pX_1,$$
$$X_3 = mX_2.$$

Note that X_2 also equals the output of the system. We can substitute and eliminate the states of the system, thereby restating the model:

$$X_2 = p(Input + X_3)$$
$$X_2 = p(Input + mX_2)$$

And since $X_2 = Output$, we have

$$Output = p(Input + mOutput),$$

or, after rearranging,

$$Output = Input[p/(1 - pm)].\qquad [2.2]$$

This derives Mason's Rule, named after its author (see Cortés et al., 1974, p. 104). Mason's Rule is a shortcut for finding the function of a single feedback loop. In words, Mason's Rule can be stated as the forward path divided by the quantity 1 minus the product of the forward path and the feedback path. Restated, Mason's Rule for determining the function of a single feedback loop is as follows:

Mason's Rule: *Forward path/*[1 − (*Forward path*)(*Feedback path*)].

This formula gets multiplied by the system's input to equal the output. The states of the system can always be used to determine the algebraic equation for any graph algebra representation. But sometimes Mason's Rule is quite handy and is introduced here as a convenience for graph algebra that a modeler may or may not wish to use.

An Example From Economics: The Keynesian Multiplier

The Keynesian multiplier is a good example from economics of the use of a positive feedback loop. Consider a system in which a nation's total income is a function of investment and consumption. Consumption acts as an additional input into the system since consumers spend their money on products, thereby reinserting their income into the functioning of the economy. Using graph algebra, we can depict such a simple economy, as in Figure 2.5.

Note that the forward path of Figure 2.5 has an element that contains the number 1. This is an "invariant transformation," which is simply an identity operation. In this model, all investments are transformed into economic output, in the sense that nothing is lost. Note also that investment and economic output are subscripted with respect to time and that the time subscript is the same for both. This means that the system is a time-dependent *simultaneous system,* in the sense that all investments are immediately counted as (or transformed into) economic output. The equation that is produced with this graph algebra representation is shown as Equation 2.3, and this can easily be obtained by applying Mason's Rule to Figure 2.5:

$$Economic\ output_t = Investment_t[1/(1 - c)],\qquad [2.3]$$

where $1/(1 - c)$ is the familiar Keynesian multiplier.

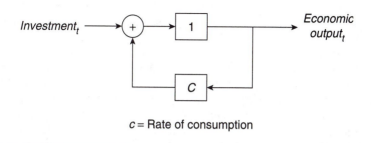

c = Rate of consumption

Figure 2.5   The Keynesian Multiplier: Economic Output as a Function of Investment and Consumption

Equation 2.3 would normally be estimated using the statistical form of Equation 2.4, where the parameter β_0 is an intercept for the statistical model and parameter β_1 is the slope:

$$Economic\ output_t = \beta_0 + \beta_1 (Investment_t) \qquad [2.4]$$

Note that an intercept could have been added to the graph algebra diagram in Figure 2.5 just as it is included in Figure 2.2. In this book, intercepts are often omitted from the graph algebra diagrams to obtain a more tidy presentation, and it is left to the reader to reinsert those intercepts in cases where desired. From Equation 2.4 we can see that $\beta_1 = 1/(1 - c)$. Thus, if we estimate Equation 2.4 and obtain the parameter β_1, then we also need to calculate the value of the parameter c, which is embedded inside β_1.

This simple example helps to emphasize a useful feature of graph algebra. Our real interest is not in finding the value of β_1, but rather the value of c. It is the graph algebra that helps us see this. If we began with the statistical model shown as Equation 2.4 (i.e., in the absence of the graph algebra representation of the role of consumption), then we might not realize that the relationship between investment and economic output is complicated by the feedback component of consumption. Thus, graph algebra assists in clarifying the specification of many such models in which the parameters of interest are embedded inside the estimated statistical parameters. In this case, the Keynesian multiplier is so well understood that one might say that the graph algebraic representation of the model is not needed. While this may be the case in this instance, there will be many other models in which the specifications are more complex and not well-known, and it is in those situations that the use of graph algebra is particularly valuable.

This example is useful in again pointing out an aspect of graph algebra that can sometimes be misunderstood. In Figure 2.5, note that an arrow leaves *Economic output$_t$* and flows through the parameter c before reentering the system at the front end of the feedback loop where the circle with the plus sign is located. This does not mean that something is being subtracted from the value of *Economic output$_t$* for it to be reentered at the plus sign. Thus, the arrow leaving *Economic output$_t$* and pointing to the parameter c is not reducing the value of *Economic output$_t$*. Rather, a measure of *Economic output$_t$* is being taken where the feedback loop begins, and some proportion (c) of this is being reinvested in the economy. Again, restated differently, the beginning of a feedback loop does not "pull" something out of the forward path. It merely takes a measure of the value of the forward path at that point in the system so that part of that measure can be reentered elsewhere in the system.

Also note that the parameter c instantaneously summarizes a set of diminishing feedback cycles, as is the case with all static and simultaneous systems. This is the same as was described previously with respect to Figure 2.4 and parameter m. In Chapter 3, we learn how to structure the feedback process using time operators, thereby keeping track of when an output actually feeds back into the system relative to other parts of the system.

3. GRAPH ALGEBRA AND DISCRETE-TIME LINEAR OPERATORS

So far time has not played a significant role in our discussions. Structuring the relationships between the variables with respect to time within the context of a system is one of the great strengths of graph algebra. All the models that are discussed throughout the remainder of this book use graph algebra to do this. This discussion begins with explaining how graph algebra is integrated with discrete-time applications. Discrete time implies the use of difference equations, and difference equations are often appropriate for the social sciences since a great deal of social scientific data are collected in discrete intervals. Examples of this are census data, economic data, election data, and polling data (which often correspond with an electoral calendar). Differential equations are used to model continuous-time processes and are discussed later. Models can also be built using graph algebra that have both continuous and discrete parts. These are called "metered" differential equations, and they are also discussed later in this book in the context of differential equations with embedded time lags.

All the operators used in this book are linear operators (see especially Allen 1963, p. 725; see also Goldberg, 1958). This is true of the discrete-time operators as well as the continuous-time operators. What do we mean by saying that these operators are linear? The condition of linearity requires that an operation satisfy two principles (see Cortés et al., 1974, pp. 293–294). The first is the principle of homogeneity. This states that if one multiplies a constant times a variable, and then applies an operator to this product, the answer will be the same if one first applies the operator to the variable and then multiplies this result by the constant. Symbolically, this is written as

Homogeneity: *Operator*[(*Constant*)(*Variable*)] = *Constant*(*Operator* [*Variable*]).

In the case of an operator of proportional transformation, we are simply multiplying by another constant. Thus, it is clear that $abY_t = baY_t$, where a and b are constants. We will want to show that the principle of homogeneity applies to the other operators presented in this book, and this is done later as those operators are introduced.

The second condition of linearity is the principle of superposition. The superposition principle is important to the study of difference and differential equations, and it is fundamental to many dynamic processes, including the superposition of states as encountered in quantum mechanics (see, e.g., Aczel, 2003, p. 85). In general, the superposition principle states that the sum or linear combination of two or more solutions to an equation is also a solution to the equation (Zill, 2005, p. 130). In the context of linear operators, applying an operator to the sum of two variables is equal to applying the operator separately to the two variables and then summing these two results. This symbolically resembles the distributive law of multiplication, in the sense that $a[X_t + Y_t] = aX_t + aY_t$. Thus, in terms of operators, we can write

Superposition: *Operator*[*Variable* 1 + *Variable* 2] = *Operator*[*Variable* 1] + *Operator*[*Variable* 2].

As with the principle of homogeneity, we will want to demonstrate that the superposition principle applies to the various operators presented in this book. Again, any operator is linear if it satisfies both these principles. Moreover, since the inverse of a linear operator reverses the functioning of that linear operator such that a variable to which the linear operator is applied is returned to its original state, inverses of linear operators are also linear operators.

Delay and Advance Operators for Discrete Time

Many social phenomena occur after some delay. That is, when a stimulus is applied, a reaction transpires at a later time. To incorporate a delay in graph algebra, a delay operator is needed. This operator is written as E^{-1}, and it is read as "E inverse." Yet other social phenomena happen in anticipation of something else that either will occur in the future or is expected to occur in the future. Thus, something happens before something else takes place. This is the opposite of a delay, and an advance operator is needed in such a situation. E^1 is the advance operator. E^{-1} is the inverse of E^1. E^{-1} changes the variable Y_t to Y_{t-1}. The advance operator (E^1) changes Y_t to Y_{t+1}. For convenience, it is conventional to write E^1 as simply E without the superscript, noting that if an advance operation is required that places a system state more than one time period into the future, then the appropriate superscript will be used, the value of which will depend on the number of time periods in question. As with delays, advance operations are a commonly encountered feature of many social phenomena. For example, when people purchase stocks on the stock market in anticipation of a future rise in the value of that stock, they are acting in advance of that expected occurrence. In a different example from the sociological literature (see Mare & Winship, 1984), some young people drop out of school in anticipation of gaining employment, while others stay in school or join the military because they anticipate a difficult time obtaining a satisfactory job. Still others may drop out of school anticipating poor employment opportunities despite a greater level of education. This can produce a self-fulfilling prophecy, a problem that may disproportionately strike young and discouraged racial minorities.

Both E and E^{-1} are linear operators. Applying the principle of homogeneity, $E[aX_t] = a(E[X_t]) = aX_{t+1}$. From the principle of superposition, we have $E[X_t + Y_t] = EX_t + EY_t = X_{t+1} + Y_{t+1}$. Similarly, with respect to E^{-1}, $E^{-1}[aX_t] = a(E^{-1}[X_t]) = aX_{t-1}$ and $E^{-1}[X_t + Y_t] = E^{-1}X_t + E^{-1}Y_t = X_{t-1} + Y_{t-1}$.

Returning to the earlier example in which campaign workers are canvassing for support by knocking on doors in a neighborhood, let us consider the campaign that occurred in Baghdad, Iraq, in January 2005. During that month, Iraqi and American officials were planning to hold elections for a new Iraqi government, and parties and politicians were actively attempting to attract support from the populace. But insurgents opposed to the American presence in Iraq were warning people not to participate in the elections (see Filkins, 2005). In this situation, the attempts of the insurgents to impose their norms on the Iraqi people would occur after a delay. First, campaign workers would interact with a potential voter. The potential voter may be influenced by this and consider supporting the candidate or party. A certain proportion of these campaign contacts would be observed by informants cooperating with the insurgents. These informants would look for evidence that the person contacted by the campaign workers might be leaning toward participating in the elections. If they suspect this to be the case, the informants would report their suspicions to the insurgents, who in turn would act to intimidate the potential voter, possibly by threatening to kill the voter and/or his or her family members. Again, this intimidation would occur after a delay, since it would take time for the informants to observe the reaction of the potential voter to the campaign stimulus and then to report this reaction to the insurgents. From a system's perspective, this is a situation that can be described in the classic terms of regulation and control associated with a delayed feedback process.

Using graph algebra, this scenario can be depicted as in Figure 3.1. Here, the input of the system is C_t, which represents the canvassing contacts that the campaign workers have with the populace, whereas the system's output is the variable V_t, which represents the result of those contacts in producing voters. In Figure 3.1, the forward path is essentially the same as it was in Figure 2.1, in the sense that the input is processed by the parameter of proportional transformation, p. However, first the input is added to a feedback path to become X_1, the first state of the system. This feedback path is called a "negative feedback loop" because of the sign of the parameter m. This parameter acts proportionally to negatively transform the output of the system (X_2) before it reenters the system. Note that the delay operator (E^{-1}) is also on the feedback path. This acts to delay the action of the feedback path by one time period.

The social interpretation of the negative feedback loop presented in Figure 3.1 is straightforward. The insurgents in Iraq calibrate their intimidation activities based on the success of the campaign workers in mobilizing new voters. As the campaign workers mobilize new voters (X_2), the insurgents will increase their intimidation. The more successful the mobilization efforts of the campaign workers, the more profound the impact of the intimidation, which algebraically means that the state of the system, X_3, will be a negative number of large magnitude. This is the classic operation of most regulation and control phenomena.

In this instance, it is heuristically useful to obtain the algebraic equation for the graph algebra diagram in Figure 3.1 both by using Mason's Rule as well as by solving for the states of the system. Beginning with the states of the system,

$$X_1 = C_t + X_3,$$
$$X_2 = pX_1,$$
$$X_3 = -mE^{-1}X_2.$$

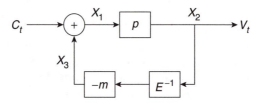

Figure 3.1   Campaign Interactions With a Negative and Delayed
Feedback Loop

As before, noting that X_2 also equals V_t, we can substitute and eliminate the
states of the system. After the first substitution we have $X_2 = p(C_t + X_3)$,
which allows us to then write this as Equation 3.1:

$$X_2 = p(C_t - mE^{-1}X_2) \qquad [3.1]$$

Substituting for X_2, we have,

$$V_t = p[C_t - mE^{-1}V_t],$$

or, after rearranging and operationalizing the E^{-1}, we have Equation 3.2:

$$V_t = pC_t - pmV_{t-1} \qquad [3.2]$$

Since it is conventional in most of the social sciences (with the exception of
economics) to write difference equations such that the lowest time script is
t and the higher time scripts are $t+\_$, we can multiply both sides of Equation
3.2 by the advance operator (E) and obtain Equation 3.3:

$$V_{t+1} = pC_{t+1} - pmV_t \qquad [3.3]$$

Equation 3.3 is a first-order linear difference equation with constant coefficients. The theory of such equations is complete (Goldberg, 1958). In economics, the convention is to write difference equations such that the highest
time script is t and all lower time subscripts are $t-\_$. If this convention was
followed here, the model would have been left in the form found in Equation 3.2. Regardless, both Equations 3.2 and 3.3 are equivalent, and one can
move from one to the other by multiplying through by either the advance
operator, E, or the delay operator, E^{-1}, as needed. Both these operators are
linear operators that obey the normal rules of algebra. Since they only work
on time-dependent variables, they have no effect on constants.

We can also obtain Equation 3.3 from Figure 3.1 using Mason's Rule. This
avoids having to work with the states of the system, and this is sometimes

more convenient. Directly applying Mason's Rule to the graph algebra diagram in Figure 3.1, we have

$$V_t = C_t[p/(1 + pmE^{-1})].$$

Rearranging yields

$$V_t(1 + pmE^{-1}) = pC_t,$$

and then

$$V_t + pmV_tE^{-1} = pC_t.$$

Now we operationalize the delay operator, E^{-1}, to produce

$$V_t + pmV_{t-1} = pC_t.$$

We then multiply throughout by E and obtain

$$EV_t + pmEV_{t-1} = pEC_t.$$

Our final form of the model is obtained after operationalizing E and rearranging to produce $V_{t+1} = pC_{t+1} - pmV_t$, which is identical to Equation 3.3.

Including an Additive Constant With Graph Algebra

Some social scientists might want to include an additive constant with the above model that would not get involved with the feedback loop, since such an additive constant would typically be employed when estimating the model using regression. There are a number of ways that this can be accomplished using graph algebra (see, e.g., Przeworski, 1975). Two different approaches to this are discussed below, the first of which is shown in Figure 3.2. The second way is easier and is discussed later. In practice, if the second way is followed, an additive constant is sometimes omitted from the graph algebraic analysis until the model is evaluated with respect to a body of data. Both these approaches can also be used to include more than just an additive constant to the model. For example, if a researcher wishes to include a function comprising a variety of control variables, linearly combined with slopes and an intercept, this can be done as well. Again, there are other ways to include functions and additive constants to a model. The two approaches described below are simply examples of how this is commonly accomplished.

In Figure 3.2, the additive constant is inserted into the model after the feedback loop. The placement of the additive constant after the feedback loop is both substantively interesting and algebraically a bit more challenging. From

26

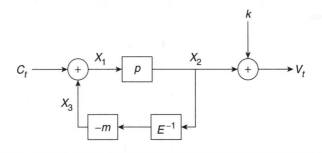

Figure 3.2   An Additive Constant Included After the Feedback Loop

a substantive point of view (continuing with the electoral campaign in Iraq example), it may be that the insurgents are responding only to personal interactions between campaign workers and the populace. That is, if the additive constant represents some additional voter mobilization process that does not originate from personal campaign interactions, then the insurgents may not react to that component of the mobilization effort. For example, the extra voter support may arise from news media broadcasts. The insurgents may not be able to monitor who is listening to the broadcasts, and therefore they may not be able to intimidate those potential voters. Thus, the feedback loop begins before the additive constant is included in the model. The algebraic complexities that result from doing this can be seen when examining the reduced-form version of the model that would ultimately be estimated using regression.

The estimated version of Equation 3.3 combined with an additive constant (omitting the error term for simplicity) is presented in Equation 3.4:

$$V_{t+1} = \beta_0 + \beta_1 C_{t+1} + \beta_2 V_t \qquad [3.4]$$

Using this form with the model shown in Figure 3.2, we have $\beta_0 = k(pm+1)$, $\beta_1 = p$, and $\beta_2 = -pm$. The formula for β_0 may at first seem strange, but it follows from the graph algebra. Return to Equation 3.1. We can no longer simply substitute V_t for X_2 since V_t now includes an additive constant that is not part of X_2. But we note that $V_t = X_2 + k$, and thus $X_2 = V_t - k$, which we can substitute into Equation 3.1. We then obtain Equation 3.5:

$$V_t - k = p[C_t - mE^{-1}(V_t - k)] \qquad [3.5]$$

Multiplying through all the brackets, we now have Equation 3.6:

$$V_t - k = pC_t - pmE^{-1}V_t + pmkE^{-1} \qquad [3.6]$$

Since m, p, and k are all constants, E^{-1} has no effect on them, and thus the delay operator can be eliminated from the last term of Equation 3.6. Rearranging, operationalizing the remaining E^{-1} with respect to V_t, and finally multiplying through by E to advance all the time scripts such that $t + 1$ is the highest scripted value yields Equation 3.7:

$$V_{t+1} = pC_{t+1} - pmV_t + k(pm + 1) \qquad [3.7]$$

It is clear now that the term $k(pm + 1)$ is simply a constant that equals β_0 in Equation 3.4. Thus, Equation 3.7 is identical to Equation 3.3, except that Equation 3.7 includes an additive constant.

After obtaining the values of β_0, β_1, and β_2, one needs to calculate the values of the parameters p, m, and k. This is a straightforward problem of normal algebra since there are three equations and three unknowns [i.e., $\beta_0 = k(pm + 1)$, $\beta_1 = p$, and $\beta_2 = -pm$]. However, the estimated parameters β_0, β_1, and β_2 are useful to us in other ways. The dynamic behavior of the model as depicted in Figure 3.2 can be determined directly through its reduced-form version, Equation 3.4. Thus, if the estimated parameter β_2 has a value between -1 and 0, then this model will display convergent oscillatory behavior over time. If the value of β_2 is less than -1, then the model will predict unstable oscillatory behavior for this system, a highly volatile outcome given the nature of the electoral dynamics modeled in this example. Other values of this estimated parameter may produce different dynamical behaviors. Readers can find complete descriptions of the dynamics of first-order linear difference equations with constant coefficients in any number of texts on finite mathematics. My personal suggestions are Goldberg (1958), Goldstein, Schneider, and Siegel (1988, chap. 11), and Baumol (1970).

Also, the equilibrium value for this model can be found by setting $V_{t+1} = V_t = V^*$, and then substituting V^* into Equation 3.4. After solving for V^*, one obtains

$$V^* = [\beta_0 + \beta_1 C_t]/(1 - \beta_2),$$

which is constant only if C_t remains stationary. Otherwise, this is a "moving equilibrium value" that is driven by the value of the system's input. For this reason, a system input is often referenced as a "driver to the system." A wider discussion of difference equation models with such characteristics can be found in Huckfeldt, Kohfeld, and Likens (1982).

Now we turn to a second approach commonly used to include an additive constant in a graph algebra model. This is shown in Figure 3.3. In this figure, the additive constant is included in the model at the beginning of the feedback loop, not after the feedback loop as in Figure 3.2. From a substantive

28

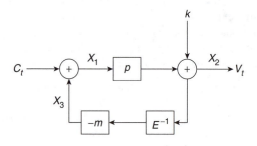

Figure 3.3   An Additive Constant Included at the Beginning of the Feedback Loop

perspective while continuing with the example of Iraqi electioneering, we may theorize that the Iraqi insurgents are keeping track of the entire vote-mobilization campaign, not just the interactions between campaign workers and potential voters. If the insurgents sense that the vote-mobilization campaign is threatening their cause through a variety of means (e.g., media broadcasts, interpersonal contacts), then they might try to suppress participation in the elections by intimidating the entire potential voting populace rather than just those interacting with campaign workers. Their strategies to broadly intimidate a populace might include more widely targeted assassinations and bombings.

Following this scenario, the repressive feedback of the Iraqi insurgents would be in response to the value of the forward path of the model plus the additive input k. This changes and simplifies the algebra when compared with the approach used in Figure 3.2. For Figure 3.3, note that $X_2 = pX_1 + k = V_t$. We begin with the statements,

$$X_1 = C_t + X_3,$$
$$X_2 = pX_1 + k,$$
$$X_3 = -mE^{-1}X_2.$$

Substituting gives us Equation 3.8, which in turn can be simplified as Equation 3.9:

$$V_t = p[C_t - mE^{-1}V_t] + k \qquad [3.8]$$
$$V_{t+1} = pC_{t+1} - pmV_t + k \qquad [3.9]$$

Applying Equation 3.4 as the reduced-form version of this model, we have $\beta_0 = k$, $\beta_1 = p$, and $\beta_2 = -pm$, which again gives us three equations and three unknowns.

Again, there are other ways of including an additive constant component into a graph algebra model. The first applied graph algebra model published in the *American Political Science Review* was developed by Przeworski (1975), and this model inserted the additive constant at the end of the feedback loop. That would be comparable to placing it at the summation point before X_1 in Figure 3.3. In one of my own published examples of a graph algebra model, an additive constant was employed following the summation of multiple forward paths (Brown, 1991, p. 191). In general, the placement of all graph algebra components depends solely on the social theory being addressed, and so specification variety across models will be the norm.

Difference and Summation Operators for Discrete Time

Up to this point, we have used only delay and advance operators to structure a model with respect to time. But some phenomena require models that take the difference of variables between two time points, accumulate values of variables across many time points, or both. The operators that do this are difference and summation operators. We treat these two operations together since they are the inverse of one another.

The difference operator is written as Δ. As with all time-structuring operators, Δ works only on time-scripted variables. By definition, $\Delta X_t = X_{t+1} - X_t$. To show that Δ is a linear operator, we need to apply the principles of homogeneity and superposition. Beginning with the principle of homogeneity, we note that $\Delta[aX_t] = aX_{t+1} - aX_t = a[X_{t+1} - X_t] = a(\Delta[X_t])$. Now with respect to the principle of superposition, we need to show that $\Delta[X_t + Y_t] = \Delta X_t + \Delta Y_t$. Note that $\Delta[X_t + Y_t] = [X_{t+1} + Y_{t+1}] - [X_t + Y_t] = [X_{t+1} - X_t] + [Y_{t+1} - Y_t] = \Delta X_t + \Delta Y_t$. Thus, the operator, Δ, satisfies the two conditions of linearity required of all linear operators.

It is quite common to model social processes that respond not to the value of a variable but rather to the change in that variable from one time point to the next. Let us return to our Iraqi elections example and say that the number of people deciding to participate in the elections from day to day is dependent not on the level of campaign contacts, C_t, but rather the change in campaign activity. The reason for this could be that voters will see the elections as a battle between those who want the elections to succeed and those who want them to fail. Seeing an increase in campaign activity may convince potential voters that those wanting the elections to succeed are prevailing in the campaign. This would embolden voters to participate on election day. On the other hand, if the level of campaign activity only stays the same or decreases, then voters may think that those who oppose the

30

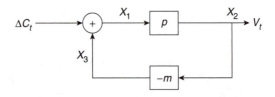

Figure 3.4   A Difference Operator in the Input to the Forward Path

elections are gaining the upper hand, dampening any sense of pro-elections momentum.

We can include the idea of change in the variable C_t in a model of the elections process as shown in Figure 3.4. In this figure, the additive constant and the delay operator have been removed to simplify the presentation. The summation operator and the delay operator will be added to the model later to show how these elements change the model's functioning.

We can use Mason's Rule to obtain the algebraic model that corresponds to the graph algebra diagram in Figure 3.4. This is shown here as Equation 3.10:

$$V_t = \Delta C_t[p/(1+pm)] \qquad [3.10]$$

Note that in Equation 3.10 the parameters p and m are both involved non-linearly with ΔC_t. When estimated, this model would produce an over-determined system of equations, since one slope estimate, say β_1, would equal $p/(1+pm)$. Thus, we would be trying to get two parameter values out of one estimated number, which we cannot do. This problem is not caused by the inclusion of the difference operator in the model. The problem is caused by the fact that the structure of the model does not separate the parameters p and m by time, as was done by including a delay operator in the feedback loop of Figure 3.3.

Rather than reintroduce the delay operator in the feedback loop, let us place a summation operator along the forward path of the model. For simplicity, let us also go back to the version in which the input is the number of daily or weekly campaign contacts, C_t, not change in those contacts. This is shown in Figure 3.5. The Δ^{-1} operator is a summation operator, and it is read as "delta inverse." It is located on the forward path of the model depicted in this figure and acts to accumulate or sum up the new voters who are being mobilized by the activities of the campaign workers, and a substantive reason for wanting to do this in a model is suggested below. But before diving into the substantive interpretation of the model, it is worth making a few observations regarding the functioning of the Δ^{-1} operator.

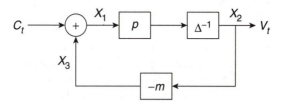

Figure 3.5   A Discrete-Time Summation Operator in the Forward Path

The two operators, Δ and Δ^{-1}, are inverse operations, in the sense that their interaction, $\Delta\Delta^{-1}$, yields the identity operation (the operator for which is I). In practice, this means that

$$\Delta\Delta^{-1}Y_t = IY_t = Y_t$$

(see Goldberg, 1958, pp. 41–44). Whereas Δ is an operator that requires that we difference a variable to yield some specified value, Δ^{-1} is an operator that requires us to find a function that will result in that same value when we difference it. Thus, if $\Delta Y_t = y_t$, where y_t is the difference and can be anything, including a constant, then $Y_t = \Delta^{-1}y_t$. The operator Δ^{-1} is the finite analog to integration with respect to the calculus. Just as integration is more challenging than differentiation in calculus, similarly performing the Δ^{-1} operation is more challenging than finding a difference using Δ. Fortunately, the property of inverse operations allows us easily to eliminate the Δ^{-1} operation in practice when using graph algebra for nearly all settings, as is explained through example below.

It is helpful to show why the operator Δ^{-1} actually accumulates over time. Let us say that Δ^{-1} transforms an input C_t into an output V_t. This can be stated as in Equation 3.11:

$$\Delta^{-1}C_t = V_t \qquad [3.11]$$

Since Δ^{-1} is the inverse of Δ, we can say that $\Delta V_t = C_t$, which is the same as $V_{t+1} - V_t = C_t$. This can be rewritten as Equation 3.12:

$$V_{t+1} = C_t + V_t \qquad [3.12]$$

Now multiply both sides of Equation 3.12 by E^{-1} to obtain Equation 3.13:

$$V_t = C_{t-1} + V_{t-1} \qquad [3.13]$$

Substitute Equation 3.13 for V_t in Equation 3.11, and you have

$$\Delta^{-1}C_t = C_{t-1} + V_{t-1}. \qquad [3.14]$$

Thus, Equation 3.14 demonstrates that the Δ^{-1} operator yields a mapping of an indefinite sum that results from having our current output (V_t, or equivalently, $\Delta^{-1}C_t$) equal to the addition of the input for the last time period (C_{t-1}) and the output for the last time period (V_{t-1}). Thus, we are taking the previous input and adding it to the previous output to get the new output. With each new iteration, we are adding one more input (from one time period only) to the previous output (which has been accumulating across all iterations), which is simply the accumulation of the input over time (see also Cortés et al., 1974, pp. 299–300).

There are many substantive reasons why we might want to model social processes using a summation operator as in Figure 3.5. Before returning to our electoral example, consider the situation of China with respect to the gender imbalance that is causing considerable stress within the population (see Yardley, 2005). There has long been a social bias favoring male children in China, which has resulted in the widespread practice of mothers opting for an abortion if the fetus is a girl. The problem is compounded by strict regulations placed on families by the Chinese government aimed at limiting population growth by reducing the number of births per couple to one. By 2005, all of this resulted in a significant imbalance between the genders, with boys outnumbering girls in some areas 134 to 100. There are long-term economic implications to this as well. The growing Chinese economy will require a stable labor force for years to come. But the reduction in Chinese fertility (defined as births per female), plus the reduced number of women available to give birth, could cause an eventual steep drop in the youthful working-age population. This gender imbalance had been slowly accumulating since the Chinese government enacted their population-control measures in the 1970s, and the government eventually reacted to the accumulated imbalance, fearing an eventual "baby bust." This is a classic situation of a feedback process that is responding not to the incremental inputs of more boys being born than girls, but to the accumulated result of these incremental inputs summed up over many years. One can use the Δ^{-1} operator to model such processes.

Returning now to an electoral example as depicted in Figure 3.5, we can say that the feedback process is responding not to the daily acts of the campaign workers interacting with potential voters, but rather the accumulated success of these contacts. This can be a general electoral process and not one relating only to the Iraqi election example used earlier. Feedback that occurs to enforce the community norms in response to a political campaign can be based on how many new voters are formed by the campaign activity over a long period of time. When the accumulated new voting support grows in the population, the community responds to repress this growth, as operationalized by the parameter $-m$, which appears in the feedback loop.

The system defined in Figure 3.5 can be expressed algebraically using Mason's Rule, as is shown in Equation 3.15:

$$V_t = C_t[(p\Delta^{-1}/(1+pm\Delta^{-1})]$$ [3.15]

Rearranging Equation 3.15 yields $V_t(1+pm\Delta^{-1}) = C_tp\Delta^{-1}$, which then simplifies to $V_t + pm\Delta^{-1}V_t = C_tp\Delta^{-1}$. Rearranging this gives us Equation 3.16:

$$V_t = C_tp\Delta^{-1} - pm\Delta^{-1}V_t$$ [3.16]

At this point, we want to eliminate the Δ^{-1} in Equation 3.16. We do so by multiplying both sides of the equation by Δ, which gives us $\Delta V_t = C_tp\Delta\Delta^{-1} - pm\Delta\Delta^{-1}V_t$. Since Δ and Δ^{-1} are inverse operations, they cancel each other, leaving us with the algebraically tractable statement found in Equation 3.17:

$$\Delta V_t = C_tp - pmV_t$$ [3.17]

Operationalizing the Δ operator as $\Delta V_t = V_{t+1} - V_t$ and then rearranging Equation 3.17 gives us our final form of the model, stated here as Equation 3.18:

$$V_{t+1} = pC_t + V_t[1 - pm],$$ [3.18]

a first-order linear difference equation with constant coefficients.

It is useful to compare Equation 3.18 with Equation 3.3 (from Figure 3.1), which is repeated for convenience below:

$$V_{t+1} = pC_{t+1} - pmV_t$$ [3.3]

Note that both the summation operator and the delay operator placed somewhere within a system containing feedback produce a first-order time-structured system. The placement of the variables in Equations 3.18 and 3.3 is the same, in the sense that both C_t and V_t appear on the right-hand sides of both equations (although note the difference in time scripts for the variable C_t in both equations). But the arrangement of the parameters is different for both equations, and this reflects differences in the social theory underlying the separate models.

It is now especially useful to see what happens if one places both a summation operator and a delay operator in the system at the same time. This could easily be justified from a substantive point of view. If the feedback reacts to the accumulation along the forward path, and if there is a delay in the activity of the feedback, we could specify our model as in Figure 3.6. In our campaign example, this might mean that the norms of the neighborhood would act to repress the success of the campaign activity after a delay. In

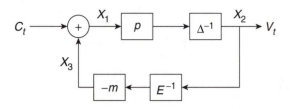

Figure 3.6   A Discrete-Time Summation Operator in the Forward Path
Combined With a Delay Operator on the Feedback Path

practical terms, neighborhood organizations would respond with their own
campaign activities that would be aimed at counteracting the original vote-
mobilization campaign, but these response activities would occur only after
the accumulated successes of the original campaign are noted by neighborhood leaders. There would be a delay in the response since it would take the
neighborhood leaders time to organize their response efforts.

Figure 3.6 can be phrased algebraically as Equation 3.19 using Mason's
Rule:

$$V_t = C_t[p\Delta^{-1}/(1 + pmE^{-1}\Delta^{-1})] \qquad [3.19]$$

Working through the algebra of Equation 3.19 is a process similar to that
used for Equation 3.15, with the exception of the inclusion of the E^{-1} operator. Rearranging Equation 3.19 yields Equation 3.20:

$$V_t + pmE^{-1}\Delta^{-1}V_t = C_tp\Delta^{-1} \qquad [3.20]$$

Rearranging, multiplying through by Δ, and then operationalizing the E^{-1}
results in Equation 3.21:

$$\Delta V_t = pC_t - pmV_{t-1} \qquad [3.21]$$

Now we operationalize the Δ on the left-hand side, rearrange, and then
finally multiply through by E to advance all the time scripts to obtain our
final version of the model, shown as Equation 3.22:

$$V_{t+2} = pC_{t+1} + V_{t+1} - pmV_t \qquad [3.22]$$

Equation 3.22 is a second-order linear difference equation with constant
coefficients. Thus, by placing both a summation operator and a delay operator within the same system loop, we increased the order of the model by one.

In Equation 3.22, the term pC_{t+1} acts to drive the second-order system in
V_t. If the campaign activity stops such that C_t goes to zero, then the output
will begin to decay gradually, as is determined by the second-order system

$V_{t+2} = V_{t+1} - pmV_t$. This is an aspect of system response (see, in particular, Cortés et al., 1974, Part 3).

A Note Regarding Additive Constants

In the previous section, I introduced the idea of including an additive constant in a model using graph algebra. Since it is possible to write a model such that an isolated constant may interact with a time operator, it is worth summarizing the observations made earlier regarding how some common time operators affect isolated constants. For example, when a delay or advance operator (E or E^{-1}) combines with an isolated constant (i.e., without the multiplicative presence of a time-dependent variable), then the isolated constant is not affected by the time operator. In such a situation, the time operator can be ignored. For example, $E^{-1}r = r$, where r is a constant. On the other hand, the difference operator, Δ, yields a zero when it interacts with an isolated constant, since constants do not change with respect to time. Thus, $\Delta r = 0$.

An Estimated Example: Labor Union Membership

It is natural to ask how one would estimate complex models that are developed using graph algebra. As can be seen with the simple examples in this chapter, the use of graph algebra can very quickly lead to models with nonlinearities in the parameters, in the sense that parameters often get multiplied by (or are otherwise combined with) other parameters. More complex graph algebra models than those shown in this chapter are also easily derived, and it should be clear that the standard approach to the linear regression model where one separable parameter exists for each independent variable in a list often will not work.

There are, indeed, a number of ways to estimate such complex models. The approaches vary in difficulty from extremely simple to quite challenging. The approach that is best for any given situation depends on the complexity of the model and, to some extent, the researcher's commitment to finding estimates for the model's parameters. If the model is highly nonlinear and complex, but it has the potential to make a big impact on a given audience, then a researcher will want to invest more effort in estimating the parameters. Sometimes this will require significant programming, and some readers may want to examine some of my own efforts in this regard (Brown, 1991, 1995a). However, very often the matter of estimating graph algebra models can be handled with little more effort than with ordinary linear regression. I work through one such example here using two separate approaches to ordinary least squares.

Let us say that we are interested in the campaign to recruit new members to labor unions that occurred in the United States from 1930 through 1970, which covers the most significant period of labor union growth in the 20th century. The data for this period are shown in Table 3.1 and are obtained from the *Historical Statistics of the United States (Millennial Edition)*. In the example worked out here, the output is labor union membership, and the input is the number of workers involved in work stoppages as a percentage of the total labor force. I explain the rationale behind using these variables in the model below. I do not use the variable for the number of work stoppages in the model, although I include it in Table 3.1 so that readers can see how the number of stoppages corresponds with the number of workers involved in the stoppages.

If one is interested in arguing that growth in labor union membership is a first-order process, where new growth comes from an expansion of the existing pool of unionized workers, then one might begin with a statistical model of an autoregressive process. This can be accomplished as with Equation 3.23. The error term is omitted for simplicity.

$$Labor_{t+1} = \beta_0 + \beta_1 Labor_t \qquad [3.23]$$

The graph algebra representation of this model is shown as Figure 3.7. Note that there are no variable inputs to the left of the system in Figure 3.7. That is, nothing outside of $Labor_t$ is driving it. The output is simply responding to itself over time via a feedback process.

We can see how well this model fits the data using a simple bivariate regression. The scatterplot of labor union membership on the lag of labor union membership is shown in Figure 3.8. For this plot, R^2 is 0.9, $\beta_0 = 1.55$, and $\beta_1 = 0.94$. Using these values and a reasonable initial condition, we can "shoot" a difference equation through the data, as is shown in Figure 3.9.

But now let us model this as a system with an input. Let us say that the growth of the labor union movement was a direct response to the activity of union members who were activists. One measure of the number of union members who are the most active in union functions is the working population that is involved in work stoppages, here measured as a percentage of the total work force. These people will be located in picket lines, for example, and many of them will be active in trying to encourage other workers to support their cause. We can think of these people as similar to the campaign activists in our previous voter-mobilization model. Using a standard statistical approach, we can incorporate this input into the graph algebra as in Figure 3.10. Our model now becomes

$$Labor_{t+1} = \beta_0 + \beta_1 \, Labor_t + \beta_2 \, Activists_{t+1}. \qquad [3.24]$$

TABLE 3.1
Labor Union Membership in the United States From 1930 Through 1970

Year	Labor Union Members[a]	Work Stoppages[b]	Activitists[c]
1930	6.8	183	0.8
1931	6.5	342	1.6
1932	6.0	324	1.8
1933	5.2	1,170	6.3
1934	5.9	1,470	7.2
1935	6.7	1,120	5.2
1936	7.4	789	3.1
1937	12.9	1,860	7.2
1938	14.6	688	2.8
1939	15.8	1,170	3.5
1940	15.5	577	1.7
1941	17.7	2,360	6.1
1942	17.2	840	2.0
1943	20.5	1,980	4.6
1944	21.4	2,120	4.8
1945	21.9	3,470	8.2
1946	23.6	4,600	10.5
1947	23.9	2,170	4.7
1948	23.1	1,960	4.2
1949	22.7	3,030	6.7
1950	22.3	2,410	5.1
1951	24.5	2,220	4.5
1952	24.2	3,540	7.3
1953	25.5	2,400	4.7
1954	25.4	1,530	3.1
1955	24.7	2,650	5.2
1956	25.2	1,900	3.6
1957	24.9	1,390	2.6
1958	24.2	2,060	3.9
1959	24.1	1,880	3.3
1960	23.6	1,320	2.4
1961	22.3	1,450	2.6
1962	22.6	1,230	2.2
1963	22.2	941	1.1
1964	22.2	1,640	2.7
1965	22.4	1,550	2.5
1966	22.7	1,960	3.0
1967	22.7	2,870	4.3
1968	23.0	2,649	3.8
1969	22.6	2,481	3.5
1970	22.6	3,305	4.7

a. Labor union membership as a proportion of total labor force.
b. Number of work stoppages.
c. Number of workers involved in work stoppages as a percentage of total labor force.

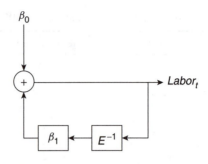

Figure 3.7   Graph Algebra of a Simple Autoregressive Process

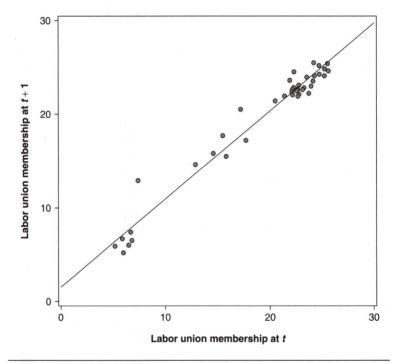

Figure 3.8   First Differences of Union Membership in the
U.S. Labor Force

Let us now model this process as we did in the voter-mobilization example
developed earlier, but with a different twist in the feedback path. Borrowing
from the earlier discussion, we can say that the success of the labor union

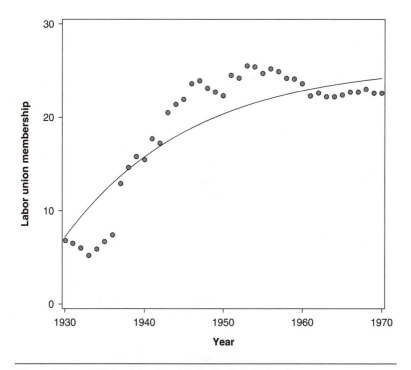

Figure 3.9   Union Membership in the U.S. Labor Force

organizing efforts will depend on the number of activists that are out there on the street trying to gain the attention of other workers. Thus, the activists themselves will be a true input that will be transformed proportionally (with respect to their own numbers) into new labor union members. But as labor union organizing efforts continue to make inroads, some proportion of those newly activated will join with the other activists to encourage workers to mobilize as well. Some of this will happen simply by the fact that the workers not yet mobilized will see the ranks of the mobilized workers growing, and they will want to join the mobilized ranks because of this. Thus, we will have a positive feedback loop, which is different from what we had in, say, Figure 3.3. This can now be depicted using graph algebra as in Figure 3.11.

The graph algebra for this model yields Equation 3.25:

$$Labor_{t+1} = \beta_0 + pmLabor_t + pActivists_{t+1} \qquad [3.25]$$

The reduced-form version of Equation 3.25 is still Equation 3.24, but now we need to determine the values of parameters p and m. By comparing

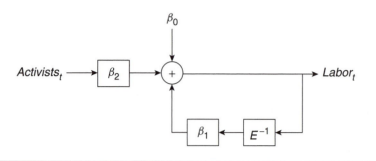

Figure 3.10   Graph Algebra of a Simple Reduced-Form
                    Autoregressive Process

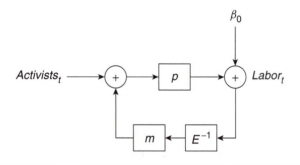

Figure 3.11   Graph Algebra of a Simple Autoregressive Process

Equations 3.24 and 3.25, we note that $\beta_1 = pm$ and $\beta_2 = p$. If we run Equation 3.24 in a multiple regression, we find that $\beta_1 = 0.944$ and $\beta_2 = 0.227$. Thus, we can now solve for the parameter on our feedback loop by dividing 0.944 by 0.227, and $m = 4.159$. The fit for this model is 0.97.

Our remaining problem is that while we do have the point estimates for our parameters, we do not yet have standard errors for those point estimates. It is important to include statistical tests for the estimated parameter values in nearly all situations. Thus, we have to use an estimation program that is different from a normal linear regression program to get the parameter estimates as well as their standard errors (and the associated P values). In many situations such as this, one can use PROC MODEL in SAS to perform this analysis easily using ordinary least squares. The exact statements that would give all the relevant statistical outputs using PROC MODEL would be as follows:

```
PROC MODEL DATA = LABOR;
ENDOGENOUS LABORUN;
EXOGENOUS LLABORUN STOPPC YEAR;
PARMS P M B;
LABORUN = (P*STOPPC) + (P*M*LLABORUN) + B;
FIT LABORUN/OLS OUT = LABOROUT OUTPREDICT;
```

In the above code, LABOR is the data set that contains the variables shown in Table 3.1, LABORUN is the unionized work force as a proportion of the total work force, LLABORUN is the lag of LABORUN, and STOPPC is the number of workers involved in work stoppages as a percentage of the total labor force. This model produces a predicted path as shown in Figure 3.12.

This example is quite simple, and researchers would normally want to specify a model of union membership growth more fully. But the basics of how to estimate many such models (or at least one approach to this) should now be clear. Another aspect that is worth mentioning is that researchers will want to check for (at least) first-order autocorrelation within the error term of the model. If this is discovered, there are different philosophies of what to do about it. One approach is to deal with it statistically (see, e.g., Ostrom, 1990). Such approaches often involve transforming the variables such that the autocorrelation is eliminated, and there are some situations in which this may be an appropriate plan of attack. But some view this approach as potentially comparable to eliminating the evidence at the scene of a crime (see Brown, 1991, pp. 203–205). If autocorrelation is present in the error term, then something systematic is escaping the model. Another way of looking at this is that autocorrelation is a sign of specification error. In situations in which one has tried all reasonable specification possibilities, then correcting the autocorrelation problem with a statistical approach may be the only option. But since graph algebra offers so much flexibility in terms of coming up with new and innovative algebraic formulations for a model, some theorists who work with graph algebra prefer to go back to the drawing board, so to speak, when faced with autocorrelation in the error term. In such situations, statistical approaches to dealing with autocorrelation are avoided, and new model specifications are derived that more effectively capture all of the systematic components that exist in the data.

With respect to working with reduced-form models, not all graph algebra models can be boiled down to a reduced-form version suitable for relatively easy estimation. But when this does happen, and if one estimates a reduced-form version of a model and then uses the parameter values for that reduced-form version (e.g., the βs in Equation 3.24) to derive the model's true parameters that are embedded within the reduced-form parameters (as with

42

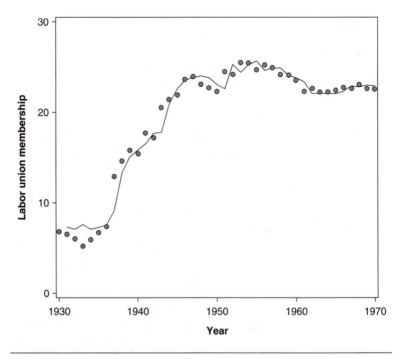

Figure 3.12   Union Membership Driven by Activists

Equation 3.25), it may be that more than one graph algebra specification can be reduced to the given reduced form. In fact, we have already seen this happen more than once in this chapter. For example, the graph algebra of Figure 3.10 produces the same reduced-form model as the one shown in Figure 3.11. Compare also Equations 3.7 and 3.9. Which one is correct when the reduced form is the same?

This is impossible to determine statistically. The correct model in this instance needs to come from social and political theory, not numbers. One works with graph algebra to translate the best theory possible into a mathematical form. After this is done, the model is sometimes reducible to a form that can be estimated using a commonly available statistical package. But as with all such models, it is the original model that is isomorphic to the theory that is being tested, and it is with the defense of that original model that a researcher would normally place his or her efforts. In a situation in which the graph algebra model stands on its own and is not reducible, the problem of competing interpretations vanishes. We will return to this issue when we examine multiple equation systems, such as Richardson's arms race model.

4. WORKING WITH SYSTEMS OF EQUATIONS

One of the great strengths of graph algebra is the ability to use the language to specify systems of equations. In most typical situations, a researcher has two or more output variables, and these variables interact either linearly or nonlinearly in a system. For example, if there are two output variables, then there would be two equations. If both variables appear in one or both equations, then the system is interdependent, which is the normal state of affairs for most systems. Social science examples of many such systems using differential equations can be found in Brown (2007), and an unusually sophisticated and fully estimated example using difference equations can be found in Przeworski and Sprague (1986). Perhaps one of the most classic of all such systems in the social sciences is the arms race model developed by Lewis Fry Richardson (1960). In this chapter, we heuristically examine Richardson's model using graph algebra. We also use graph algebra to explore alternative interpretations of this model.

Richardson's Arms Race Model Using Graph Algebra

Richardson originally presented his arms race model as a system of two differential equations. However, others have also explored this model using difference equations (see, especially, Huckfeldt et al., 1982, pp. 45–65). In this chapter, I also express this model in terms of difference equations. Interested readers can find an introduction to this model using continuous-time mathematics in Brown (2007).

Three simple premises underlie the algebra of Richardson's arms race model (see Richardson, 1960, pp. 13–16). First, a nation spends more on weapons when it observes that other nations are spending more on weapons. Second, military spending is an economic burden to society, and greater levels of spending will inhibit future increases in spending. Third, grievances and ambitions relating to both cultures and national leaders either encourage or discourage changes in military spending. All of this can be summarized algebraically as

$$\Delta x_t = a y_t - m x_t + g, \qquad [4.1]$$

$$\Delta y_t = b x_t - n y_t + h, \qquad [4.2]$$

where a, m, g, b, n, and h are constant parameters of the model. Here we have two nations, X and Y. Changes in their respective spending on arms are represented by Δx_t and Δy_t. The positive terms $a y_t$ and $b x_t$ represent the drive to spend more on arms due to the level of spending of the other

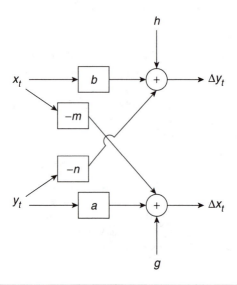

Figure 4.1 A Graph Algebra Representation of Richardson's Arms Race Model

nation, and the negative terms mx_t and ny_t reflect the desire to inhibit future military spending due to the economic burden of current spending. The constants g and h represent the grievances and ambitions of the leaders for nations X and Y, respectively.

The simplest way of expressing Equations 4.1 and 4.2 using graph algebra is presented in Figure 4.1. Here we have two forward paths beginning with x_t and y_t and ending with Δx_t and Δy_t. However, note the crisscrossing paths that connect x_t and y_t through the negative parameters m and n to the alternative forward paths. With this way of writing the model using graph algebra, there are no obvious feedback paths, and the model appears to be composed of interdependent forward paths that are added together. However, this is not entirely true, as I explain below.

A close reading of Richardson's own description of the specification of his model (Richardson, 1960, pp. 13–16) suggests that he was indeed thinking of a feedback process when he discussed the negative influences on the economy of continued arms spending. Indeed, one popular treatment of this model explicitly describes this model as having a feedback process (Huckfeldt et al., 1982, p. 45). Thus, it is normal to ask why we do not see a feedback loop in Figure 4.1 if there is a feedback process.

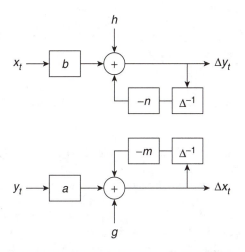

Figure 4.2   Alternative Graph Algebra Representation of Richardson's Arms Race Model

To see how this feedback process works using graph algebra, it is necessary to rewrite the model as presented in Figure 4.2. In Figure 4.2, the feedback loop is now apparent, and this representation yields the same result as that presented in Figure 4.1. The Δ^{-1} operator is needed on the feedback path to cancel the Δ operator feeding into this path from the output.

It is useful to note that the feedback process shown in Figure 4.2 is a special type of feedback process. Consider a microphone being used by a speaker in an assembly. In the presence of feedback, a presenter talks into the microphone, and the signal is then processed through an amplifier before manifesting as an amplified voice that comes out of the system's speakers. The sound from the speakers then reenters the presenter's microphone and is reamplified by the system before coming out (again!) from the system's speakers. That is, the sound is processed twice by the same system. This type of feedback is called a "primary" feedback system.

A careful examination of the system presented in Figure 4.2 reveals that the feedback loop does not reenter the system at the beginning of the forward path, to be processed (again) by the parameter b. Indeed, the feedback from the output (without the Δ) is simply proportionally transformed and re-added to the output. Going back to the microphone example, this would be comparable to having some of the sound signal coming from the system's speakers reenter the system through the wires leading to the speakers, thus bypassing the rest of the system (i.e., the microphone and the amplifier) entirely. This type of feedback is called a "secondary" feedback process to differentiate it from a primary feedback process that inserts the feedback into the front end of the system for reprocessing. Thus, Richardson's arms race model contains a secondary feedback process.

Variations of Richardson's Arms Race Model

One of the great strengths of using graph algebra is the ease with which scientists can modify their mathematical specifications to more closely match their theoretical ideas. If one's reading of Richardson's verbal rationale for including a feedback process involving economic burden leads to thinking that perhaps he was really considering a primary rather than a secondary feedback process, then one would want to specify this explicitly in the model. Alternatively, perhaps one might simply want to know what the arms race model would look like with a primary feedback process regardless of an interpretive reading of Richardson's original ideas. Either way, the task is easily accomplished by rearranging Figure 4.2 as is done in Figure 4.3. We will call this our alternative interpretation #1 of Richardson's arms race process.

With Figure 4.3, the feedback process reinserts the output (after cancelling the differencing and applying a proportional transformation) to the forward path prior to any processing by the system. Substantively, this suggests that nations change their armament spending after jointly considering the competing power's spending and their own economic burden. Thus, national leaders would balance these two competing influences on their spending decisions as one lump sum. As Richardson's model is originally specified (Figures 4.1 and 4.2), the national leaders consider the competing power's spending independently of their economic burden. If nation Y increases spending by so much, then nation X will want to change its own spending by a certain amount as a response to this. The economic burden does not enter into this part of the calculation. But in Figure 4.3, the economic burden does enter into the original calculation of how heavily to weigh the impact of a competing power's spending on arms. If this is how a theorist views the arms race process, then Figure 4.3 is a more accurate representation of this.

The algebraic representation of the graph algebra shown in Figure 4.3 is given here as Equations 4.3 and 4.4:

$$\Delta x_t = ay_t - amx_t + g \qquad [4.3]$$

$$\Delta y_t = bx_t - bny_t + h \qquad [4.4]$$

Note how these equations differ from Equations 4.1 and 4.2. In Equations 4.3 and 4.4, the model is now nonlinear in parameters. This has direct

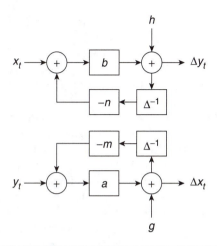

Figure 4.3   Alternative Interpretation #1 of Richardson's
Arms Race Model

implications with respect to estimating the parameter values for this system. If we want to know the value of parameter a in Equation 4.3, we simply have to estimate the model and note the value of the parameter that is multiplied by the term y_t. But if we want to know the value of parameter m, it is not so easily done.

Let us now work with the reduced-form version of Richardson's arms race model, and this is shown as Equations 4.5 and 4.6:

$$\Delta x_t = \beta_1 y_t - \beta_2 x_t + \beta_3 \qquad [4.5]$$

$$\Delta y_t = \beta_4 x_t - \beta_5 y_t + \beta_6 \qquad [4.6]$$

This reduced form is isomorphic to Richardson's original algebraic specification of the arms race process. In other words, based on the respecification portrayed in Figure 4.3, Richardson's original specification was actually a reduced-form version of the arms race process. If Equations 4.3 and 4.4 represent our real thinking of this process, then we note that $\beta_1 = a$, $\beta_2 = am$, $\beta_3 = g$, $\beta_4 = b$, $\beta_5 = bn$, and $\beta_6 = h$. This is a system of six equations and six unknowns. We can estimate the system's reduced-form parameters using normal statistical software. But once we find our values of β_i, we then need to use these values in the six equations above to determine the values of a, m, g, b, n, and h. This is easily done since, in this case, only parameters m and n require any algebraic manipulations to obtain their values. But the theoretical point is crucial. With Richardson's original algebraic specification, once we find the values for parameters β_i, we are done with estimating the system. But now we see that the parameters m and n are buried inside the reduced-form parameters β_2 and β_5, which requires us to do an additional step to dig them out, so to speak. (This also has implications with respect to evaluating the confidence intervals for the embedded parameters, a subject that is discussed by way of an example below. But see also the appendix in Brown, 1995a, for a detailed discussion relevant to more complicated situations.)

Another way to think about Richardson's arms race process involves the constant terms h and g. Why should the grievances and ambitions of the national leaders be included in the tail end of the model? Might it not be possible that these elements would be considered simultaneously in one lump sum with the competing nation's arms spending and the economic burden, much as was done in Figure 4.3? If this is the thinking of the theorist, then it might be better to write the model as shown in Figure 4.4. We can call this our alternative interpretation #2 of Richardson's arms race process.

In Figure 4.4, all the inputs and the feedback are inserted in the front end of the model. Here we are again working with a primary feedback process, and a nation adjusts its spending on arms after a joint and weighted (because of the parameters of proportional transformation) evaluation of (1) the competing nation's overall arms spending, (2) the economic burden of current arms spending, and (3) the grievances and ambitions of the leaders. The algebraic translation of Figure 4.4 is shown here as Equations 4.7 and 4.8:

$$\Delta x_t = ay_t - amx_t + ag \qquad [4.7]$$

$$\Delta y_t = bx_t - bny_t + bh \qquad [4.8]$$

With this specification, our reduced-form parameters, β_i, now correspond with the following mapping: $\beta_1 = a$, $\beta_2 = am$, $\beta_3 = ag$, $\beta_4 = b$, $\beta_5 = bn$, and $\beta_6 = bh$, which is again six equations with six unknowns. In this instance, four of the reduced-form parameters have more than one embedded model parameter, and each instance requires an additional algebraic step before one has finished estimating the model. More specifically, we need to find the value for parameter a before we can find values for parameters m and g, and we similarly need to find the value for parameter b before we can find values for parameters n and h.

Let us modify the specification of Richardson's original arms race model once again to incorporate the idea that change in the arms spending for nation X is not due to the level of arms spending for nation Y, but rather the difference between the spending for the two nations. This can be represented as shown in Figure 4.5.

In the front end (i.e., left-hand side) of Figure 4.5, note that the crisscross pattern of the inputs produces a subtraction of the level of one nation's arms

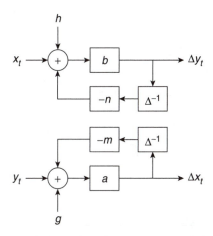

Figure 4.4   Alternative Interpretation #2 of Richardson's
Arms Race Model

spending from the other. Thus, our resultant inputs are the difference between the nations' arms spending, not the total level of spending for each nation. Note also that I have placed a delay operator on both forward paths. I have added this to represent the idea that change in a nation's spending will be lagged by 1 year due to the normal budgetary calendar. Thus, an increase in arms spending by one nation in one year will cause a spending response by the other nation the next year. This delay is not mandatory by any means. But it is an interesting possibility, and I include it here for heuristic consideration.

The algebraic translation of the graph algebra shown in Figure 4.5 resolves to Equations 4.9 and 4.10:

$$\Delta x_{t+1} = ay_t - (1+m)ax_t + ag \qquad [4.9]$$
$$\Delta y_{t+1} = bx_t - (1+n)by_t + bh \qquad [4.10]$$

This is now an interdependent system of two second-order difference equations with constant coefficients. Now our reduced-form parameters, β_i (from a second-order version of Equations 4.5 and 4.6), correspond to the following mapping: $\beta_1 = a$, $\beta_2 = (1+m)a$, $\beta_3 = ag$, $\beta_4 = b$, $\beta_5 = (1+n)b$, and $\beta_6 = bh$, which again is six equations with six unknowns. The model can still be estimated in reduced form using standard statistical software, and the embedded parameters from the model can still be determined from the six equations above. But now the embedded parameter specification is not at all obvious without the accompanying graph algebraic pictorial representation.

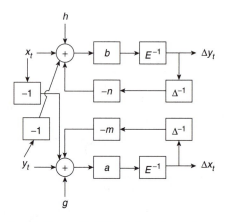

Figure 4.5   Alternative Interpretation #3 of Richardson's
Arms Race Model

Finally, readers might note that the theory presented in Figure 4.5 is beginning to look quite a bit like an electric circuit diagram. This has become more the case as we have incrementally added specification nuances to the model. This superficial similarity betrays the system theory origin of graph algebra. Readers might also note how different Figure 4.5 is from, say, Figure 2.2, which is a graph algebraic representation of a linear regression model. Comparing Figure 4.5 with Figure 2.2 is useful on another level. One reason why electric circuit diagrams are more complicated than many social scientific models is that electrical engineers have long had a schematic language with which to structure their ideas. In large part, graph algebra addresses the need for social scientists to have a similarly flexible language with which to specify complex social scientific theories.

In short, graph algebra is a language that encourages a relatively easy reconciliation between social theory and algebraic specification in many situations. How far a theorist wishes to push this reconciliation depends on the practical and theoretical needs of the theorist for any given social scientific research problem.

An Estimated Example of a Multiple-Equation System With Nonlinear or Embedded Parameters: Richardson's Arms Race

As in Chapter 3, we are interested in knowing that our graph algebra models can be estimated. Again, there are numerous ways to estimate models with nonlinear or embedded parameters. The approach used in this section is just one of many, and I encourage readers who want to go farther in this area to read works where numerically intensive methods are used to estimate highly complex model specifications in both discrete and continuous time (see, e.g., Brown, 1991, 1995a; Hamming, 1971, 1973 [Hamming, 1971, is particularly useful]).

For this example, we will use Richardson's arms race model, first as specified by Equations 4.1 and 4.2, and then as specified by Equations 4.3 and 4.4. In both cases we will decompose the Δ operator so that the higher-order term can be isolated on the left-hand side (although estimating the left-hand side as a difference is also possible, of course). We begin with Equations 4.1 and 4.2, which are (from the perspective of this chapter) the reduced-form version of Richardson's model. Rearranging Equations 4.1 and 4.2 so that the higher-order terms are on the left-hand side gives us Equations 4.11 and 4.12:

$$x_{t+1} = ay_t + x_t(1 - m) + g \qquad [4.11]$$

$$y_{t+1} = bx_t + y_t(1 - n) + h \qquad [4.12]$$

First, we need to choose parameter values and then to generate data using these equations. For this demonstration, the following parameter values are used in Equations 4.11 and 4.12: $a = .2, m = .3, g = .1, b = .1, n = .5, h = .1$. Using these parameter values, the model is iterated 40 times and the data set shown in Table 4.1 is generated. The equilibrium values for the model with these parameter values are $x^* = .538$ and $y^* = .308$. The estimation process described below also works if one adds random noise to the data values, although there will be some (expected) variation in the estimated parameter values and the fit of the model depending on the amount of noise added.

An easy way to estimate this model is to use PROC MODEL in SAS. Again, there are other methods, and not all methods work equally well. PROC MODEL does a fairly decent job using ordinary least squares in the current situation as long as the data do not have large amounts of noise. Different numerically intensive methods can work better under conditions of significantly larger amounts of noise. Employing PROC MODEL to estimate Equations 4.11 and 4.12, the following SAS code could be used:

```
PROC MODEL DATA = armsrace;
ENDOGENOUS x2 y2;
EXOGENOUS x1 y1;
PARMS a m g b n h;
x2 = (a*y1) + x1*(1 − m) + g;
y2 = (b*x1) + y1*(1 − n) + h;
FIT x2 y2 / OLS OUT = armsout OUTPREDICT;
```

TABLE 4.1
Simulated Richardson's Arms Race Model Values

Time	X	Y
1	1.00000	0.70000
2	0.94000	0.55000
3	0.86800	0.46900
4	0.80140	0.42130
5	0.74524	0.39079
6	0.69983	0.36992
7	0.66386	0.35494
8	0.63569	0.34386
9	0.61376	0.33550
10	0.59673	0.32912
11	0.58353	0.32424
12	0.57332	0.32047
13	0.56542	0.31757
14	0.55931	0.31533
15	0.55458	0.31359
16	0.55092	0.31225
17	0.54810	0.31122
18	0.54591	0.31042
19	0.54422	0.30980
20	0.54292	0.30932
21	0.54191	0.30895
22	0.54112	0.30867
23	0.54052	0.30845
24	0.54005	0.30828
25	0.53969	0.30814
26	0.53941	0.30804
27	0.53920	0.30796
28	0.53903	0.30790
29	0.53890	0.30785
30	0.53880	0.30782
31	0.53872	0.30779
32	0.53866	0.30777
33	0.53862	0.30775
34	0.53858	0.30774
35	0.53856	0.30773
36	0.53853	0.30772
37	0.53852	0.30771
38	0.53851	0.30771
39	0.53850	0.30770
40	0.53849	0.30770

In this code, x2 and y2 are the variables X and Y in Table 4.1, and x1 and y1 are their lagged values. When the above code is used on the original variables (i.e., without noise), the exact parameter values are obtained as output, and the fit of the model is unity.

Now let us estimate Richardson's arms race model as I have respecified it using Equations 4.13 and 4.14, both of which have the higher-order terms on the left-hand side (compare with Equations 4.3 and 4.4):

$$x_{t+1} = ay_t + x_t(1 - am) + g \qquad [4.13]$$

$$y_{t+1} = bx_t + y_t(1 - bn) + h \qquad [4.14]$$

In these equations, all the parameters remain in the model, but they are arranged differently as compared with Equations 4.11 and 4.12. Now we want to estimate the parameter values in their new arrangement using the same data as before (i.e., Table 4.1) using Equations 4.13 and 4.14.

The SAS code used to estimate the new model is now:

```
PROC MODEL DATA=armsrace;
ENDOGENOUS x2 y2;
EXOGENOUS x1 y1;
PARMS a m g b n h;
x2 = (a*y1) + x1*(1 – a*m) + g;
y2 = (b*x1) + y1*(1 – b*n) + h;
FIT x2 y2 / OLS OUT=armsout OUTPREDICT;
```

Using this code, the estimated parameter values are as follows: $a = .2$, $m = 1.5$, $g = .1$, $b = .1$, $n = 5$, and $g = .1$. The fit of the model is unity, as again would be expected in the complete absence of noise. The new parameter values now reflect the new specification. Thus, if our theory really corresponds with the ideas conveyed by Equations 4.3 and 4.4, but we naively estimate the model using Equations 4.1 and 4.2 (not realizing this is a reduced-form version of the correct model), then the high fit of the empirical results could lead us to accept the parameter values as estimated and to misunderstand the arms race process. We need to specify the model as in Equations 4.3 and 4.4 to obtain parameter values that accurately reflect our theory.

5. APPLYING GRAPH ALGEBRA
TO CONTINUOUS TIME

Graph algebra works with both discrete and continuous-time models. So far, we have explored the use of graph algebra using difference equations and difference operators. But if one wants to work with differential equations, there are clear analogies between the difference and differential modalities that are worth noting. In this chapter, I discuss some of the analogies between differential calculus and the calculus of finite differences. This not only helps explain how differential equations may be modeled using graph algebra but also assists in working with nonlinear difference equations, a topic that is continued in the next chapter.

To begin, the difference operator, Δ, in discrete time is analogous to a derivative in continuous time. Thus, Δy_t is analogous to dy/dt. From the definition of the derivative,

$$\frac{dy}{dx} = \lim_{h \to 0} \frac{y(x+h) - y(x)}{h} = \lim_{h \to 0} \frac{\Delta y(x)}{h},$$

where the variable x is substituted for t for generality. The derivative dy/dx is the slope of the line that is tangent to the curve for y at point x. Moreover, the line that connects the two points on the curve y that correspond with the values $(x+h)$ and x has the slope $\Delta y(x)/h$. The relationship between this slope and the derivative is the basis of all the analogies between differential calculus and their difference equation counterparts.

A list of all the analogies that are appropriate to the current context between differential calculus and the calculus of finite differences can be found in Goldberg (1958, pp. 46–49). However, a few of the analogies are nonobvious, and it is worthwhile to dwell on them here since they will be useful to us later. We begin with the product rule for differentiation. The derivative of the product of two functions, $u(x)$ and $v(x)$, is the well-know result

$$\frac{d(uv)}{dx} = u\frac{dv}{dx} + v\frac{du}{dx}. \qquad [5.1]$$

The difference analog for the above rule is derived as follows:

$$\Delta[u(x)v(x)] = u(x+h)v(x+h) - u(x)v(x) \qquad [5.2]$$

Let us now add and then subtract the term $v(x)u(x+h)$ from the right-hand side of Equation 5.2 to obtain Equation 5.3:

$$\Delta[u(x)v(x)] = u(x+h)v(x+h) - v(x)u(x+h) \\ +v(x)u(x+h) - u(x)v(x) \qquad [5.3]$$

Collecting our terms, we now have

$$\Delta[u(x)v(x)] = u(x+h)[v(x+h) - v(x)] + v(x)[u(x+h) - u(x)]. \qquad [5.4]$$

Since $u(x+h) = E(u)$, where E is the advance operator, we can rewrite the right-hand side of Equation 5.4 to arrive at Equation 5.5:

$$\Delta[u(x)v(x)] = Eu(x)\Delta v(x) + v(x)\Delta u(x) \qquad [5.5]$$

Equation 5.5 is the difference analog to the product formula given above as Equation 5.1. The nonobvious aspect of Equation 5.5 is the presence of $Eu(x)$ on the right-hand side instead of simply $u(x)$, as might be presumed by guessing the solution after examining the differential counterpart, Equation 5.1. Note that Equation 5.5 equals Equation 5.1 in the limit as $h \to 0$. The finite formula (Equation 5.5) may sometimes be of use when manipulating some situations involving nonlinear difference equation models specified using graph algebra, a subject of the next chapter.

Using similar steps as outlined above, it is straightforward to develop the finite difference counterpart to the division rule for differential calculus. In particular, the division rule for differential calculus is the familiar form,

$$\frac{d(u/v)}{dx} = \frac{v(du/dx) - u(dv/dx)}{v^2}. \qquad [5.6]$$

The finite difference counterpart to Equation 5.6 is Equation 5.7:

$$\Delta \frac{u(x)}{v(x)} = \frac{v(x)\Delta u(x) - u(x)\Delta v(x)}{v(x)Ev(x)} \qquad [5.7]$$

As with Equation 5.5, the nonobvious element is the presence of the advance operator in the divisor of the right-hand side of Equation 5.7. While I do not go through the steps here to develop Equation 5.7, they can be easily accomplished by the reader and are similar in nature to those used to develop Equation 5.5.

Using Graph Algebra With Continuous-Time Operators

It is often possible to translate difference equation models into differential equation models by substituting differential calculus operators for their difference counterparts. In the most simple of cases involving models containing only the difference operator, Δ, one can simply substitute the derivative for the differenced variable. For example, Richardson's original arms race model can be written in differential equation form as Equations 5.8 and 5.9. Indeed, Richardson himself specified his model in continuous time.

$$dx/dt = ay - mx + g \qquad [5.8]$$
$$dy/dt = bx - ny + h \qquad [5.9]$$

Graph algebra versions of this model are shown here as Figures 5.1 and 5.2, which are the continuous-time versions of Figures 4.1 and 4.2, respectively. To construct Figure 5.2, it is necessary to replace the Δ^{-1} operator found in Figure 4.2 with an integral sign. Since integration is the inverse

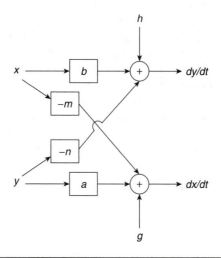

Figure 5.1 A Continuous-Time Version of Richardson's Arms Race Model

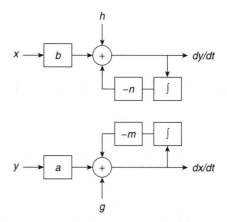

Figure 5.2 Alternative Continuous-Time Representation of Richardson's Arms Race Model

operation of differentiation, the integral sign is needed to transform the output (which is a derivative) into one of the state variables (i.e., x or y) for use in the secondary feedback path. Sometimes users of graph algebra use the symbol D^{-1} instead of the integral sign to indicate the taking of the integral or antiderivative. If this is done, it also makes sense to use D instead of dx/dt to indicate differentiation. The choice of notation is up to the user.

Delay and advance operators have no continuous-time analogs. Nonetheless, these operators can be used directly within differential equation models. In the case of the delay operator, E^{-1}, this can be used to construct a differential equation model with lags, which would be a metered differential equation. Such equations can exhibit highly nonlinear behaviors over time and are discussed in greater depth in the next chapter.

This chapter has not introduced the topic of how to analyze differential equation models once they have been developed using graph algebra. Readers wanting an introduction to differential equation modeling as related to the social sciences might wish to consult Brown (2007).

6. GRAPH ALGEBRA AND NONLINEARITY

There are an endless variety of ways that one can work with nonlinear models using graph algebra. Indeed, assisting in the specification of nonlinear models is one of the greatest strengths of using graph algebra. One should always remember that there are two types of nonlinearity. The first is nonlinear longitudinal behavior, and all but the most trivial of dynamic models can produce this. The second is functional nonlinearity, and this is where the model itself contains nonlinear terms, such as X^2 or XY. The first type of nonlinearity can be produced by functionally linear and functionally nonlinear models, and readers can find a longer discussion of this type of nonlinearity in Brown (2007) (see also Brown, 2008). This chapter develops a number of general specification strategies for working with the second type of nonlinearity, functional nonlinearity. These strategies are useful in many practical settings involving nonlinear models.

In normal circumstances, functional nonlinearity is achieved using graph algebra by using a variable as an operator of proportional transformation. This means that instead of putting a constant parameter in a box used in a system, one puts a variable. It is typical for all input variables in a system to be accompanied by a constant parameter of proportional transformation along the path that leads to the output. But when a variable is used in a box along the same path, a constant parameter is normally included as well. An exception to this can occur when the variable being used as an operator of proportional transformation changes in a deterministic manner. These ideas are best introduced by way of examples.

Nonlinear Filters

Nonlinear filters have been productively used in social scientific research, and they are an excellent entry point to incorporating functional nonlinearity into a model using graph algebra. Their application is best shown via an example. Cortés et al. (1974, pp. 251–254) suggest a modeling strategy for working with the idea of socialization as a means of absorbing tensions in a society that can be widely applied in numerous and diverse settings. If tensions are the input into a society and, say, riots or other forms of dissent are an output, then one might want to be able to model how socialization can absorb (i.e., filter) those tensions before they become transformed into an output. One way to do this is to use a parameter that decreases in value as a society matures. Thus, new democracies may be more susceptible to violent dissent among its citizens who do not yet trust the democratic institutions of governance to resolve their concerns. But as the democratic government ages and gains more experience in resolving such concerns, the citizens may be more likely to work within the boundaries of the established governing system without resorting to dissent outside of those boundaries.

The function presented as Equation 6.1 captures this idea:

$$S_t = S_0 + S_1^{t+1}, \qquad [6.1]$$

where S_t is the ability of a society to absorb tensions, and S_0, S_1, as well as their sum S_t, are between 0 and 1. At time $t = 0$, S_t is equal to $S_0 + S_1$, which allows the highest quantity of tensions into the system. When $t > 1$, the value of S_t decays to S_0.

A graph algebra model that describes this theory is presented as Figure 6.1. In this figure, the variable S_t resides on the forward path between the input and the remainder of the system, which in this case includes a feedback path. Thus, the input needs first to get through the filter, S_t, before it can be processed by the bulk of the system. Any tensions (the input for the model) that do not get through S_t are absorbed by the society and do not enter this latter part of the system. Since the filter is itself variable, and it gets multiplied by the input, it is a nonlinear filter.

Figure 6.2 shows how S_t decays to the value of S_0 over time. If we are modeling a newly formed democracy, the value of S_t would be assumed to be rather large (when t is relatively small) and many of the tensions in society will move into the remainder of the forward path on the route to the system's output. But as time moves forward, S_t will reduce in size and fewer of these tensions will survive past S_t, as portrayed with graph algebra in Figure 6.1.

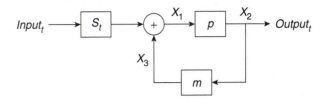

Figure 6.1   A Variable Operator of the Proportional Transformation
Can Make a System Nonlinear

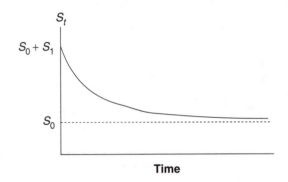

Figure 6.2   A Function Can Be Used to Describe Change in a
Parameter, $S_t = S_0 + S_1^{t+1}$

The algebra of this model is processed in the normal manner regardless of whether or not there is a variable operator of proportional transformation in the system. Thus, from Figure 6.1 we have Equation 6.2,

$$Output_t = Input_t S_t \left(\frac{p}{1 - pm} \right). \qquad [6.2]$$

Equation 6.2 produces higher levels of output when t has smaller values and lower levels as t grows larger. Due to the changing nature of S_t, this model is functionally nonlinear.

The Logistic Function

One of the most important and broadly useful of nonlinear functional forms is the logistic equation, and it is particularly helpful to examine its structure

60

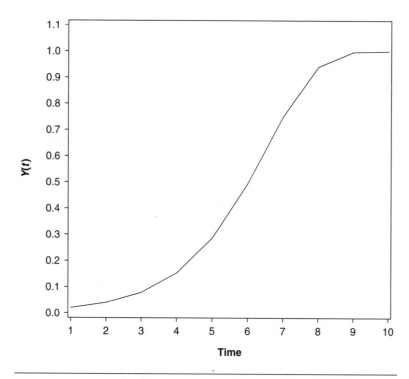

Figure 6.3   The Logistic Different Equation With $a = 1.02$, $Y(0) = .02$

from the perspective of graph algebra. I work with the logistic function as a difference equation below, but readers may be interested in a related discussion of the logistic form as a differential equation that can be found in Brown (2007). There are many ways to write the logistic equation, but a general form of this model is $\Delta Y_t = a Y_t (1 - Y_t)$, where a is a constant parameter of the model and 1 is the limit for Y_t. For computational purposes, this equation may be written as $Y_{t+1} = a Y_t (1 - Y_t) + Y_t$. This equation produces the familiar S-shaped curve shown in Figure 6.3. It is clear from Figure 6.3 that Y_t approaches its equilibrium value of 1 as time increases.

A graph algebra representation of the logistic model is shown as Figure 6.4. This is not the only way to write the graph algebra for this model. A fast way of reading such models from their graph algebra is sometimes simply to note that the two paths that meet at the summation symbol both get multiplied by the parameter a on the forward path, yielding $\Delta Y_t = a(Y_t - Y_t^2) = a Y_t (1 - Y_t)$. Note that the Δ^{-1} operator is needed on the feedback path to cancel (as an inverse operation) the Δ that feeds into the feedback path from the

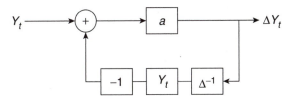

Figure 6.4   A Graph Algebra Specification of the Logistic Model

output. Note also that functional nonlinearity arises from having the variable Y_t as an operator of proportional transformation on the feedback path.

Mason's Rule also works in decomposing Figure 6.4 into an equation, but special care needs to be taken in working with linear operators in nonlinear models. Using Mason's rule, we have

$$Y_t \left(\frac{a}{1 + aY_t \Delta^{-1}} \right) = \Delta Y_t,$$

which then yields

$$aY_t = \Delta Y_t + aY_t \Delta^{-1} \Delta Y_t = \Delta Y_t + aY_t Y_t = \Delta Y_t + aY_t^2.$$

Note that the Δ^{-1} operator does not apply to the aY_t that precedes it. (See below for additional discussion of how to work with operators in nonlinear models.) This then produces

$$\Delta Y_t = aY_t - aY_t^2 = aY_t(1 - Y_t),$$

our final result.

Another way of representing the logistic model using graph algebra is shown as Figure 6.5. In this instance, I have inserted a variable limit U_t into the model. There are many instances in which this might be useful. Let us say that we are modeling population growth using a logistic model. There might be reasons why the limit of the population would vary over time. For example, if we are investigating the global human population, the limit for this population may depend on advances in agricultural technology with respect to the production of food. But we can turn this example around (in a negative sense) and say that the limit might depend on the destruction of the environment due to global warming. Filling this idea out a bit, some climate models suggest that the polar ice caps may melt in future decades due to global warming, and some have suggested that this could lead to a significant rise in sea levels. If the rise is sufficiently large, this could force the abandonment of many coastal cities, including (using the United States as

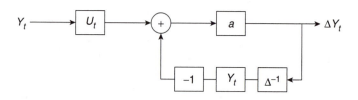

Figure 6.5   A Graph Algebra Specification of the Logistic Model With a Variable Limit

an example) New York, Miami, Los Angeles, San Francisco, Washington, D.C., Seattle, Houston, etc. This could result in huge population migrations inland. Since so much agricultural land is located along the coastal regions, there could also be risks of food shortages. These shortages could be compounded by more severe weather, a long-predicted result of global warming. The list of possible dire consequences due to global warming can go on and on. But the point to be made here is that we might want to associate the planet's population limit to, say, the level of global warming.

In Figure 6.5, note that the variable limit acts directly on the input into the system. One can decompose this model using Mason's Rule as in Equation 6.3:

$$\Delta Y_t = Y_t U_t \left(\frac{a}{1 + aY_t \Delta^{-1}} \right) \qquad [6.3]$$

Rearranging yields Equation 6.4:

$$\Delta Y_t = aY_t(U_t - Y_t) \qquad [6.4]$$

From Equation 6.4, it is clear that the limit, U_t, can now vary, and the value of Y_t will "chase" that limit asymptotically over time.

Cortés et al. (1974, pp. 257–259) suggest yet another way of using graph algebra to specify Equation 6.4. Their version, which I have adapted to discrete time, is presented here as Figure 6.6. Readers are encouraged to compare Figure 6.5 with Figure 6.6 closely to see how graph algebra can often be variously arranged to yield the same algebraic result. This is common to systems theory in general, and readers will note that there similarly are numerous ways to diagram most electrical circuits such that each version achieves the same final result.

Delays and Instability

The logistic model can also be expressed in terms of continuous time. Rather than simply substitute continuous-time operators for discrete-time

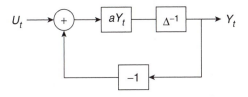

Figure 6.6 An Alternative Graph Algebra Specification of the Logistic
Model With a Variable Limit

operators in a graph algebra representation of the logistic model, let us also
add a delay to the continuous-time version. Delays, in general, can introduce significant levels of dynamic nonlinear instability to a model. A useful
introduction to this type of nonlinear instability can be found in Haberman
(1977, pp. 162–169). In terms of the logistic model, let us say that change in
a population does not respond to its current numerical levels. Rather, the
population responds to past levels of its aggregate numbers. For example,
let us say that one is modeling population growth as a function of environmental decay that is caused by the population itself. Environmental decay
typically takes some time to become noticeable. Using the example of the
ozone hole caused by the release of chlorofluorocarbons into the atmosphere, it typically takes about 12 years for those airborne chemicals to
travel from the Earth's surface to the stratosphere where the ozone damage
occurs. Thus, the damage that occurs today was caused by the human population 12 years ago. If we want to capture this delay in our model, we need
to rewrite the logistic model such that it responds in contemporary time not
to the present conditions, but past conditions.

Algebraically, this is accomplished as is shown in Equation 6.5:

$$\frac{dY_t}{dt} = aY_t(1 - Y_{t-i}), \qquad [6.5]$$

where the value of i indicates the length of delay. Note that the delayed term
Y_{t-i} occurs only in one part of the right-hand side. The part in parenthesis
acts to describe the influence of the past values of the dependent variable on
the current value of the derivative. As the value of Y_{t-i} approaches its limit
(in this case set at unity), the derivative, dY_t/dt, approaches zero. Time
subscripts are used in this continuous-time model to differentiate the values
of Y at time t from those that are delayed (i.e., Y_{t-i}).

To incorporate a delay such as expressed in Equation 6.5 using graph
algebra, we need to use the delay operator, E^{-i}, where again the $-i$ indicates the length of the time delay. In discrete time, the value of i is always
an integer value. But with continuous time, the length of delay can be any

64

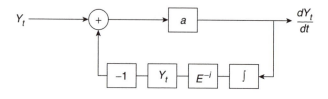

Figure 6.7   A Graph Algebra Specification of the Logistic Model With a Delay

real number. One strategy for the specification shown as Equation 6.5 is presented in Figure 6.7. This is a good example of why it is important to be careful in the application and placement of linear operators in nonlinear models. Note in Figure 6.7 that the delay operator is on the feedback path, and in terms of the direction of flow on that path, it follows the integral sign and precedes the variable Y_t. This placement is essential. It says that the system's output, dY_t/dt, that is at the beginning of the feedback path first encounters $\int$, which transforms dY_t/dt into Y_t due to the nature of inverse operations. The result of this, Y_t, then encounters the delay operator, E^{-i}, which transforms Y_t into Y_{t-i}. This result, Y_{t-i}, then multiplicatively encounters Y_t, which then results in Y_tY_{t-i}, which then gets multiplied by -1 before being added to the input, Y_t, at the summation sign. This results in the algebra shown in Equation 6.6:

$$\frac{dY_t}{dt} = a(Y_t - Y_tY_{t-i}) = aY_t(1 - Y_{t-i}) \qquad [6.6]$$

The instability that is introduced into the model when using delays is apparent in Figure 6.8, which corresponds with Equation 6.6. Here, $a = 3$, and the delay (i) is 0.2 on the time scale. Note that the smooth asymptotic approach to the limit that is shown in Figure 6.3 is now replaced with oscillations around the equilibrium. In this case there is oscillatory convergence to equilibrium, but parameters and delays could have been set such that greater levels of nonlinear instability would result.

Placement Rules for Operators in Nonlinear Models

When working with nonlinear models, it is particularly important to take care with regard to how one uses time operators. There is little risk of making an algebraic error with linear models, since the operators described in this book (such as E^{-1}, E, Δ, and Δ^{-1}) will connect with only one variable at a time in such models. But with nonlinear models, an operator can

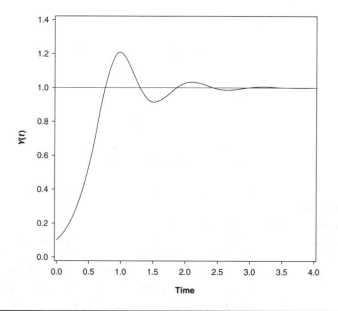

Figure 6.8   The Logistic Model With a Delay

multiplicatively "bump" into a term containing more than one variable, and one needs to know if the operation will affect all variables or just one of the variables.

The basic rules to follow begin with noting the direction of flow for each path in question. Then keep track of the sequence in which the operators interact with the variables. For example, consider the two paths shown in Figure 6.9. For Path #1, the graph algebra resolves to Equation 6.7, whereas for Path #2, the graph algebra resolves to Equation 6.8:

$$Path\#1\text{: } V_t = \Delta(C_t U_t) = C_{t+1} U_{t+1} - C_t U_t \qquad [6.7]$$

$$Path\#2\text{: } V_t = (\Delta C_t) U_t = (C_{t+1} - C_t) U_t \qquad [6.8]$$

With Path #1, the multiplication of the variables C_t and U_t happens before the encounter with the difference operator Δ. Thus, the difference operator affects the product of the two variables as if that product is one item. But with Path #2, the difference operator encounters the variable C_t first, and thus it operates only on that variable before interacting muliplicatively with the variable U_t. Previously, we have similarly encountered this idea when dealing with the logistic function as defined using graph algebra. The order of operations matters with nonlinear systems, and one cannot rearrange

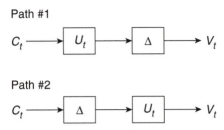

Figure 6.9   Examples of Path Flow and Operator Precedence

operators in nonlinear contexts as if they obey the commutative property of multiplication.

In linear situations, the operators described in this book are analogously commutative, although it is technically more accurate to say that they satisfy the property of homogeneity as described in Chapter 3. For example, $\Delta E y_t = E \Delta y_t$, also $\Delta a y_t = a \Delta y_t$, where a is a constant (see Goldberg, 1958, p. 36). Indeed, the operators E^{-1}, E, Δ, and Δ^{-1} are called *linear* operators because they analogously obey the commutative and distributive laws in linear contexts. With regard to analogously obeying the distributive law, it is more accurate to state that the operators satisfy the property of superposition, as is also described in Chapter 3 of this book. The point being made here, however, is that the homogeneity and superposition properties of linear operators do not apply to the nonlinear context. In nonlinear situations, modelers need to keep track of the direction of the path flows and the precedence of the operators with respect to these flows.

A related situation deserving attention here involves how two inverse operators affect the same variable when the variable appears twice multiplicatively. For example, it should be noted that

$$\Delta Y_t \Delta^{-1} Y_t \neq \Delta \Delta^{-1} Y_t.$$

The reasoning behind this can be easily seen through the analogy of continuous time. The multiplication of a derivative and an integral is not the same as the derivative of an integral. The first is an authentic multiplication of two different things, whereas the second is the mutually destructive operation of two inverse operations. For example, consider the simple function $f(x) = y = x$. Note that $f'(x) = 1$, and $\int f(x)dx = \frac{1}{2}x^2 + C$, where C is the arbitrary constant of integration. Now,

$$dy/dx \int f(x)dx = 1\left[\frac{1}{2}x^2 + C\right] = \frac{1}{2}x^2 + C. \qquad [6.9]$$

However, we also note that

$$\frac{d \int f(x)\, dx}{dx} = x,$$

[6.10]

a different result from that of Equation 6.9.

To summarize, the order in which operations occur in graph algebra in the context of nonlinear models is crucial. In general, when an operator appears on any path (forward or feedback) in nonlinear systems, it should be applied only to whatever precedes it with respect to the flow of the path.

Graph Algebra and Chaos

Graph algebra is a language that can be used in an exploratory manner to develop new nonlinear model specifications that may be associated with chaos and other complex behaviors. For example, perhaps the most famous of all continuous-time models used to study chaos involves the "strange attractor" discovered by Lorenz (1963). The three equations of that model are shown here as Equations 6.11, 6.12, and 6.13:

$$dx/dt = s(y - x)$$ [6.11]
$$dy/dt = rx - y - xz$$ [6.12]
$$dz/dt = xy - bz$$ [6.13]

In this system, the three state variables are x, y, and z, whereas s, r, and b are parameters of the model. This model was originally investigated as a means of exploring weather patterns. The system is interdependent, since the variables appear in more than one equation. It is also an autonomous system, since the independent variable t is not included explicitly in the model.

When developing a model such as this, the theorist is confronted with the challenging problem of having to figure out, on the level of algebra alone, how change in one variable will be affected by both the levels and the change in other variables. Many social theorists may find it helpful when working with nonlinear processes to exploit a graph algebra schematic picture of these processes, thereby extending the algebraic flexibility of their efforts. The graph algebra representation of this model is presented here as Figure 6.10. In this model, the manifestation of chaotic behavior is due to the model's nonlinear structure and the choice of parameter values.

Figure 6.10 shows just how complex the structure of Lorenz's model actually is. For example, there are both linear and nonlinear paths, such as the two paths from the variable x to the output for dy/dt. There is also a relative difference in the model when x is subtracted from y before being

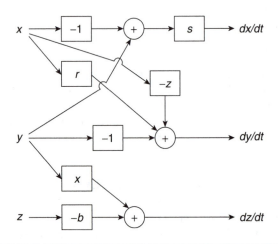

Figure 6.10   The Chaos Model Due to Lorenz

multiplied by parameter *s*, yielding the output *dx/dt*. All told, there is a lot going on with this model, and graph algebra helps to manage the various paths. In this case, we are starting with Lorenz's model and subsequently adding graph algebra to it as a means of understanding the specification. But most modelers will want to work with graph algebra from the beginning since it helps in the original conceptualization and creative processes.

To see how complex such a nonlinear process can become, it is useful to examine one of the many possible outcomes of Lorenz's model. Figure 6.11 is a phase diagram for Lorenz's model. Here we have the sequential path (called a "trajectory") of the three state variables without the representation of time. (A more detailed discussion of this type of plot can be found in Brown, 2007.) This is a snapshot of the strange attractor of the Lorenz model. Once a trajectory from the model arrives in the neighborhood of this attractor, it forever orbits in irregular and nonrepeating patterns around the two zero vectors that reside in the middle of the pretzel-shaped holes of the attractor. This is a deterministic model, but it behaves as if it is stochastic in many respects.

A great deal of research is currently being conducted on chaotic systems such as this one. Indeed, the general subject of nonlinear differential and difference equations is a rare area of mathematics in which undergraduates can encounter cutting-edge research on a level that is accessible to them. Chaos theory, catastrophe theory, and the more general study of nonlinearity and its applications are a few examples of such research. Moreover, it is likely that some of the most exciting future research in the social sciences will come from investigations of similarly nonlinear dynamic models, and the language

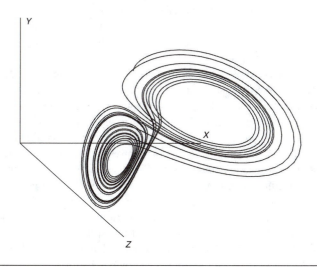

Figure 6.11   The Strange Attractor of the Lorenz System

of graph algebra has great potential in assisting these investigations (see, in particular, Kiel & Elliott, 1996; see also Richards, 2000). A discussion of the highly complex dynamics of Lorenz's model as well as a more general discussion of chaos can be found in a number of sources, including Brown (1995b).

Forced Oscillators

A particularly useful way to introduce nonlinearity into a model using graph algebra is by including what is known as a "forced oscillator." Forced oscillators are quite common in models of physical systems, and the topic of forced oscillators appears often in texts addressing the use of differential equations to model such systems (see Brown, 2007; see also Blanchard, Devaney, & Hall, 2006, p. 382). They are typically used in situations in which a system responds to an input or stimulus that varies in a regular or recurring fashion. For example, the movement of a pendulum can be modeled using a forced oscillator. Sometimes these are called "forced harmonic oscillators" or "forced equations."

Social and political systems can often be modeled using forced oscillators. For example, elections in democratic countries typically occur every few years at regular intervals. In the United States, congressional elections occur every 2 years, and presidential elections occur every 4 years. We also experience many other aspects of our lives in cyclical patterns, such as when we eat, sleep, and exercise. Our economies go through somewhat regular cycles of growth and decline. We go to work daily, take vacations yearly, and go to worship services weekly. In short, humans are periodic creatures in many respects.

There is more than one way to insert periodic behavior into a model using graph algebra. One approach is to let a parameter vary with a given periodicity. For example, we can change Richardson's arms race model to incorporate cyclical electoral behavior. Let us say that one of the nations in the arms race is a democracy that has regular, periodic elections. It could be that the leaders of the political parties for that nation (especially the incumbent parties) find that scaring their country's citizens with fearful ideas relating to the potentially hostile nature of the other nation is a good way of getting votes. In some cases, a leader may even initiate or increase hostile military actions prior to an election. Since elections happen periodically, scary speeches and associated increases in military spending of this sort may coincide with the electoral calendar. One way to incorporate these ideas into a modified specification of Richardson's arms race model is shown in Figure 6.12.

In Figure 6.12, the term describing the grievances and ambitions (previously parameter h) of the leaders for nation Y is now

$$h + q\left[.5 + \frac{\sin(pt)}{2}\right].$$

While there are a variety of ways to specify an oscillatory input, this specification is useful because of the ease with which the parameter values may be interpreted. This input function allows the input value to vary between h and $h + q$. From the theory outlined above, in periods corresponding with the electoral calendar for nation Y, this input should rise to a maximum level of $h + q$. Subsequent to this, the value of this input should reduce to h. This is an example of sinusoidal forcing. The period of the input is $(2\pi)/p$, which is the same as saying its frequency is $p/(2\pi)$.

Figure 6.12 resolves to Equations 6.14 and 6.15:

$$\Delta x_t = ay_t - mx_t + g \qquad\qquad [6.14]$$

$$\Delta y_t = bx_t - ny_t + \left(h + q\left[.5 + \frac{\sin(pt)}{2}\right]\right) \qquad\qquad [6.15]$$

The model is now nonautonomous because the independent variable, t, is explicitly included. Readers interested in these types of models may find the discussions by Blanchard et al. (2006, pp. 397–407) and Brown (2007) of interest. It is also useful to note that we could have placed the forcing term elsewhere in the model. For example, rather than include forcing with parameter h, we could have specified parameter b to include forcing,

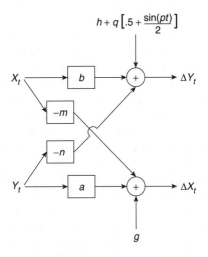

Figure 6.12   Richardson's Arms Race Model With a Forced Oscillator
Tied to an Electoral Calendar

perhaps due to the fact that nation Y may respond to military spending by
nation X (i.e., not grievances and ambitions on the part of the leaders, which
would be parameter h) in a manner correspondent with an electoral calendar. To include this with graph algebra, the entire forcing term (similarly
specified as with the above discussion relating to parameter h) would be
included in the box currently containing parameter b in Figure 6.12. Readers may find Danby's (1997, pp. 102–106) discussion of this type of forcing
to be particularly interesting. Although he applies the forcing within the
context of a predator-prey model, his approach to modeling is broadly
applicable to a variety of settings.

7. WORKING WITH CONDITIONAL PATHS

Throughout this book, we have been working with systems that have fixed
paths. That is, none of the paths turn on or off depending on particular internal or external conditions. Sometimes it may be useful to develop a model
using graph algebra in which certain conditions trigger a path to activate or
deactivate. Paths that are active only under certain conditions are conditional
paths. They can arise in a great many contexts, and my discussion in this
chapter addresses only a few potential applications.

The idea of using conditional paths is closely related to the concept of "scope conditions" that is frequently mentioned in the context of theory building in sociology. Original work in this area dates back to Toulmin (1953). However, more recently scholars have added greatly to the overall theoretical framework that applies to scope conditions (see, especially, Cohen, 1980, 1989; Liao 1990, 1992; Walker & Cohen, 1985). The basic idea of scope conditions is that certain theories or theory fragments only apply when certain conditions are met. For example, there can be a relation between two variables (or, in our current context, states of the system that are connected by a path), x and y, and we can reference that relationship using the notation xRy. We want to develop the most generalizable theory possible, but universal generality may not be possible. In the social sciences, many phenomena or relationships occur under certain restricted conditions, and we can note that these phenomena or relationships are reliably replicable when those restricted conditions are met. When applicable restrictive conditions are relaxed, the probability that any given phenomenon or relationship manifests is reduced. In the theory-building process that follows, the researcher attempts to find the limits under which the given phenomenon or relationship may manifest by relaxing the restrictive conditions incrementally until the phenomenon or relationship no longer reliably occurs. At that point, one can posit that the boundaries of the system within which the phenomenon or relationship may reliably manifest are defined.

Using the notation that often appears in the sociological discussions, we can say that a given relation between two variables can be expected if a certain scope condition is satisfied, or $SC1 \rightarrow xRy$. For our purposes, we can think of this relation, xRy, as identifying a path between two states of a system and that this path exists as an operable entity only if a given scope condition is satisfied. This allows us to build our theories to be as complex as needed by stating when and under what conditions certain paths may operate. We can move our theories in the direction of generalizability by continuing to test the boundaries of the scope conditions.

Conditional paths can be used in many disciplinary and theoretical settings. As a heuristic approach, I offer an example below showing how conditional paths can be used with logical and decision theory, a very active field of research in the social sciences.

Logical and Decision Systems

A great deal of work has been done in the social sciences in the area of decision (or "choice") theory. Much of this falls under the categories of game theory, social choice, and, more broadly, rational choice theory. It is useful at this point to discuss briefly how graph algebra might be used in this area since this may be an area of application for some readers. So far in this book, the discussion has focused on synchronic change. As mentioned previously, synchronic change as a modal process is invariant as long as the system continues to operate. Diachronic change is the opposite, and this essentially dictates that the system is no longer valid, and a new system has taken its place. Some discussions of logical and decision systems have focused on exploiting diachronic change by specifying two approaches. One is where two or more related but nonetheless different systems are described separately, and the other is where the paths of one system are conditional and would operate only if certain conditions present themselves (Cortés et al., 1974, pp. 261–267). Let us turn now to the second approach in which one might put two systems together by making one or more of the paths conditional.

Let us reconsider Richardson's arms race model from the perspective of a conditional path. The model as it was originally developed has each country in the arms race worried about the other country. But let us say that one country is a democracy (Country A), and this country's military spending is only raised in response to the military spending of the other country (Country B) when a political party with an aggressive military agenda (e.g., a "rightist" party) is leading the democratic government (in Country A). When a less aggressive party wins power, the arms race essentially stops. We can graph this dynamic relationship by modifying Figure 4.1 to contain a conditional path as shown in Figure 7.1.

In Figure 7.1, the top-most forward path is represented with a dashed line, and this is the conditional path. It is my preference to use solid lines for fixed (invariant) paths and dashed, dotted, or dashed-dotted lines for conditional paths. With such systems, a conditional path only becomes active when some condition or decision occurs. The activation of a conditional path can operate like a computer program with various conditional statements, such as "if-then" statements. If the condition or decision occurs, then the path operates in the normal manner. If the condition or decision does not occur, then the path is inactive.

It is also possible to create paths that are only partially inactivated or activated, depending on the triggering condition or decision. For example, it may be that the democratic country described above does not ignore the arms race entirely when a less aggressive party assumes power. Rather, the less aggressive party becomes less concerned about the arms race as it focuses more heavily on, say, domestic concerns and spending. In this case, the path remains, but its impact on the system varies depending on the political ideology of the party in power. This is still a conditional path; it is just that the path has more flexibility in its operation than a simple binary on/off switch.

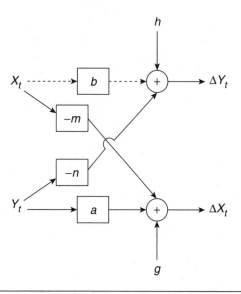

Figure 7.1   A Conditional Path in Richardson's Arms Race Model

This example can fall under the category of choice theory because choice theorists can develop their own theories for path activation. That is, choice theorists can develop theories (say, by proving theorems) that would specify under what conditions the path would activate, either partially or fully. In this sense, a choice theory can dynamically interact with a systems theory. During the functioning of the choice theory, the systems theory responds to this functioning, and the choice theory can subsequently respond to the new "facts on the ground" as determined by the operation of the system. This dynamic back and forth action that is possible between a choice theory and a systems theory can result in highly sophisticated theoretical constructs.

An Example of Democratic Transition

Let us now further develop these ideas of conditional paths using a different example and an alternative algebraic approach, one that does not use dashed lines in the graph algebra. In the early part of the 21st century, China's nominally communist government was ruling over a fast-growing capitalist economy. As this economy continues to grow, pressures build up within China to modernize its government with democratic institutions so as to encourage continued economic growth. Indeed, it is possible that the personal involvement (on the level of ownership) of the nation's own leadership with the capitalist economy will encourage thinking of democratic modernization as an economic necessity to protect their own wealth and investments. If one is modeling Chinese governance using graph algebra, how would one incorporate the transition from authoritarian to democratic rule? Stated differently, if it is the choice of the Chinese elite to choose a democracy over authoritarian rule, how does one use graph algebra to model this choice?

Using conditional paths with graph algebra, it is possible to specify a pathway algebraically such that its influence on the system is described mathematically rather than by using a logical or decision mechanism. Since it is possible to describe transitions mathematically, it is possible to use graph algebra to model transitions. The way one does this ultimately depends on the preferences of the modeler, since there is no one way to model most situations. Thus, what I offer here is an example, not a recipe.

One way to approach the transition from authoritarian rule to democratic governance is to build a catastrophe model that describes the level of centralization within the government. A democratic government is more decentralized than an authoritarian government; the latter tends to emphasize top-down decision making and hierarchical control. If one conceives of a democracy as a government in which decentralization is significantly greater than in an authoritarian government, then one can think of each government as residing on the ends of a continuous scale measuring the level of centralized control. What we now want is a way to describe rapid change from one end of that scale to the other. Catastrophe theory can do this. Moreover, it can do this within the context of one synchronic model. That is, it is possible to use graph algebra to specify a catastrophe theory model that allows for sudden governmental change without having to abandon one model and design another, even though the change in governance appears diachronic in nature.

While it is not possible to describe catastrophe theory in significant detail here, readers can find accessible descriptions of its prominent features in Brown (1995b, 2008), fully developed and estimated social scientific examples in Brown (1995a), an application of catastrophe theory to the subject of marriages in Gottman, Murray, Swanson, Tyson, and Swanson (2003), and a classic ecological example in Ludwig, Jones, and Holling (1978). There also exists a broad mathematical literature on catastrophe theory that is highly relevant to the present discussion cited in many of the above references.

Catastrophe theory works by establishing competing equilibria within one model. Each equilibrium has its own basin of attraction, or area within the model's phase space for which each equilibrium is dominant. As a consequence, a trajectory of the model that crosses the threshold separating the the different basins of attraction will suddenly be drawn toward one of the competing attractors (i.e., equilibria). With respect to a particular trajectory, sequence of events, or history, this indicates that the model has experienced the disappearance of one attractor and its basin and the sudden appearance of another attractor and its basin. This event leads to dramatic change within the system.

For catastrophe models to work, there needs to be something called a "control parameter." A control parameter is a parameter that can vary incrementally. Change for this control parameter is described as part of the system, and there usually is a separate equation that describes this change. When the value of this control parameter passes a threshold level (called a "bifurcation point"), the system experiences rapid change as trajectories "fly" from one attractor to another. One possible approach to modeling change in this control parameter is to model the sequence of choices faced by governmental leaders as they trade off the benefits of a continuation of the authoritarian government (perhaps in terms of leadership stability, otherwise known as "safe seats" in democratic parlance) as compared with the potential economic benefits that would arise from more modern democratic institutions, which would include, say, a modernized judiciary that would be able to settle corporate disputes.

There is a large literature on dynamic games, some of which use differential equation modeling. Such approaches might be used to specify change in the control parameter. Thus, we would have a complex system that would blend assumptions of rationality with sequential choices leading to a threshold that would have dramatic overall consequences for systemic governance. On the one hand, graph algebra can be used to model the theory's general form with respect to establishing competing attractors, and on the other hand, dynamic choice modeling can be used to move around within the system. This combination of environmental structure and dynamic choice modeling results in bifurcation passage and change in governance. Here we do not have a purely rational world absent evolutionary determinism, nor do we have a purely deterministic world absent rationality. Rather, we have rational interaction with competing deterministic potentials, which is an interesting form of hybrid modeling. It would not be difficult to add probabilistic aspects to this interaction as well, leading to a highly sophisticated theoretical construct.

In the above example, catastrophe theory is used to vary the influence of a path by building into the model a method by which a parameter's value swings rapidly from one value to another. In terms of its influence on the values of the system's variables, this approach is similar in effect to the approach used earlier (in Figure 7.1) in which graph algebra is used to specify the logical conditions under which certain paths may apply in the model. The conditional path approach moves the modeling enterprise farther toward the realm of diachronic modeling, as suggested by Cortés et al. (1974, pp. 261–267). But the catastrophe approach allows for the system to be described as a truly synchronic model, thereby eliminating the need to separately code the paths with either continuous or dashed lines. Both approaches are equally useful and appropriate in treating model pathways that act conditionally.

Again, these are only examples of how theorists might want to use graph algebra to specify change. I tend to view social change as a complex mixture of individual choice and stimulus-response determinism that is environmentally linked, all of which is mixed with a healthy dose of true stochasticism, and these examples reflect this hybrid perspective. But graph algebra is a neutral modeling language, not a perspective. How theorists actually use graph algebra will be determined not by my examples, but by their own modeling needs.

8. SYSTEMS, SHOCKS, AND STOCHASTICITY

Social systems rarely run smoothly for long. Always something comes along that stresses the system. We can think of this stress as a recurring stochastic element within our system that is governed by the laws of probability. But we can also think of this in terms of a single and clearly definable shock to our system. These stochastic concepts can be built directly into a model using graph algebra, and it is important to consider the theoretical implications with respect to where the stochastic elements are included.

Let us reconsider the logistic function with a delay, including stochasticity into the model, in two separate ways. First, let us add the idea that our population limit may be subject to stochastic variations. Thus, we have a limit that is composed of two factors: (1) a deterministic limit that is a single scalar and (2) variations around that limit that are due to stochastic factors outside of our system. Our deterministic component is actually the mean of the stochastic limit. For example, let us say that we are using the logistic function to model the population of a geographical area, but that significant variations in the weather (caused by things such as global warming or a storm that wipes out a season's crops) affect the food supply for extended periods of time. Thus, the population level of the area will tend to track toward whatever limit exists, but the limit never stays still.

One possible graph algebraic representation of this idea is that shown in Figure 8.1. Note that the stochastic element is now part of the system. Such

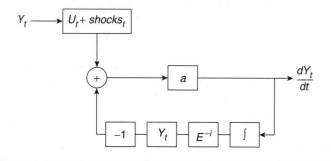

Figure 8.1   A Graph Algebra Specification of the Logistic Model With a Delay and Shocks

elements can be inserted into both discrete- and continuous-time models in a similar fashion.

While it is easy to move from a graph algebraic representation of a model (such as Figure 8.1) to an algebraic representation of the same model, analyzing the algebraic representation can become quite challenging in the case of nonlinear models, especially when the models include stochastic elements. The "problem" is that graph algebra eases the development of even very complex models, which is the great strength of graph algebra. But once one has such a model, one needs to consider how to analyze it. The most challenging cases involve continuous time, and legacy approaches to these types of problems include complex integration schemes and Laplace transformations. Fortunately, the age of fast computers has brought with it a collection of relatively simple solutions to these types of problems. When working with continuous-time models, a growing number of mathematicians now recommend the use of numerical methods (such as a fourth-order Runge Kutta) to solve for these systems. An explanation of how to do this (with numerous examples relevant to the social sciences) can be found in Brown (2007).

The time series graph of the continuous-time model shown in Figure 8.1 is presented in Figure 8.2. As with all time series graphs of continuous-time models presented in this book, numerical methods were used to obtain the values of the state variables (in this case, Y_t). For Figure 8.2, a normally distributed stream of shocks with a mean of 0 and a standard deviation of .3 was added to U_t. It is clear from this figure that the value of Y_t is attempting to follow this moving target. Sometimes a theorist may want to apply a "hammer blow" to the system rather than a continuous stream of stochasticity, and this would differ from the steady stream approach used to construct Figure 8.2. A hammer blow would be a single shock from which the

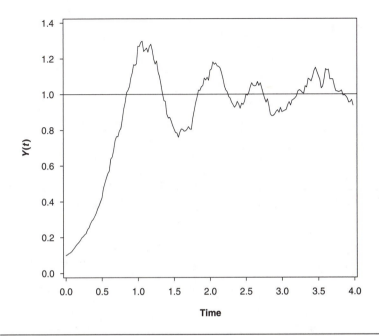

Figure 8.2   The Logistic Model With a Delay and Variable Limit

system would have to recover. In such a case, the graph algebra could be the same as in Figure 8.1, but the resultant time series plot would differ.

Let us also consider the case in which stochasticity is added to the growth parameter of the logistic model while continuing to work with the delayed logistic equation. The graph algebraic representation of the model is now shown as Figure 8.3.

Figure 8.4 is one example of a time-series plot for this model. As before, a numerical method (a fourth-order Runge Kutta) is used to compute the values of Y_t, a surprisingly easy task despite the complexity of the model (again, see Brown, 2007). Here, a stream of random, normally distributed variations with a mean of 0 and a standard deviation of .4 was added to the value of parameter a. Such a model with a variable growth parameter and delays can exhibit wildly complex longitudinal behavior. This particular simulated example is actually one of the more sedate versions from which I had to choose for inclusion here.

Stochastic elements as either random streams or single hammer blow shocks are especially appropriate for simulations of a system. This information is useful for exploring how a system behaves under stressed conditions,

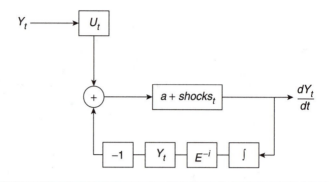

Figure 8.3   A Graph Algebra Specification of the Logistic Model With a Delay and a Variable Growth Rate

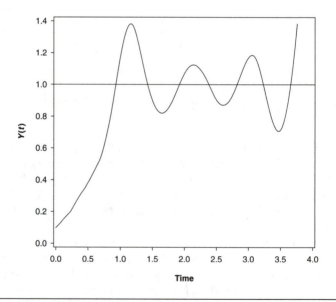

Figure 8.4   The Logistic Model With a Delay and Variable Growth Rate

where the modeler is able to control the degree of stressing. But sometimes a modeler will want to include the stochasticity in the form of actual data. This would be particularly useful in situations in which a parameter can have a conditional value, which means that the value of the parameter can

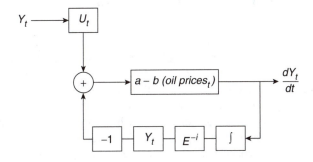

Figure 8.5 A Graph Algebra Specification of the Logistic Model With a Delay and Variable Growth Rate That Is Dependent on Oil Prices

be one value in the absence of the influence of a chosen variable but some other value after accounting for this variable's influence. One approach to this is to make a parametric element in the system a linear function of one or more variables. (For fully estimated social science examples of this approach, see Brown, 1995a.)

Let us consider a situation in which the population growth rate depends on the price of oil. Oil is used for many things that could affect a population's ability to grow. For example, in addition to using oil to power farm machinery and to transport produce and people, oil is also used in the manufacture of many fertilizers. If a theorist wants to consider the impact of oil prices on population growth using the logistic model, one approach could be that shown in Figure 8.5.

In Figure 8.5, no random shocks are added. Rather, we now have a forward path that includes the linear function $a - b(oil\ prices_t)$. The negative sign in front of parameter b is a result of the expectation that higher oil prices would lower the population growth rate. Graph algebra makes it tempting (and easy) to continue increasing the complexity of this model by adding a hammer blow shock to this linear function, which could reflect a sudden increase in oil prices that might occur in the case of, say, another war in the Middle East. The linear function might then be $a - b(oil\ prices_t) - c(shocks_t)$, all of which would be inserted in the box on the forward path of Figure 8.5. The algebraic representation of this model is shown as Equation 8.1:

$$\frac{dY_t}{dt} = [a - b(oil\ prices_t) - c(shocks_t)]Y_t(1 - Y_{t-i}) \qquad [8.1]$$

9. GRAPH ALGEBRA AND SOCIAL THEORY

Nearly everything that occurs in the universe can be considered a part of some system, and that certainly includes human behavior and, potentially, human attitudes as well. But this does not mean that systems theory, and thus graph algebra, is appropriate for use in all situations. There are many competing approaches to the study of social and political phenomena, and systems theory using graph algebra is only one such approach. All approaches to scientific investigation carry some theoretical baggage, and it is useful to pause a moment to consider the theoretical content of systems theory as it has been presented in this book.

The use of graph algebra implies some specific theoretical content that is independent of the theorist. That is, the language of graph algebra is theory-driven from the start, and when one uses this language, one embeds one's own theory with that which arrives automatically bundled with the language. What is this bundled theoretical content?

To understand the theoretical content that is implied with the use of graph algebra, let us compare its use with the empirical approach of the linear regression model. The value of a linear regression model can be found predominantly in the statistical significance of its component variables. Thus, the emphasis with a linear model is on the components of the model, not on the model as a whole. With a linear model, we have a list of independent variables, and we are interested in the relative correlations between these variables and the dependent variable. We want to know which variables influence change in the dependent variable the most. But with systems, the components cannot be considered independent of the whole. With systems, we are not interested in the components except in terms of their role as elements of a system. Rather, we are interested in the activity of the system, and we want to conduct our investigations such that the activities as a whole can be understood. This implies that people or things act as inputs into a system, and then that system operates according to its own internal logic. As a consequence of this operation, the system produces an output. The system's operation thus acts to transform the inputs into outputs. This means that when we study societies using systems, we are examining the process of transformation, a point made forcefully by Cortés et al. (1974, pp. 271–272).

What then is the system that acts to transform an input into an output? The system is defined by its structure, and the system's structure engages in activity. This activity is the function of the system. Thus, the activity itself is not the system; it is the "life" of the system. But is the social theory of the system wedded to the system's structure, its activity, or both? Let us consider this question indirectly by comparing the rational choice and stimulus-response approaches to theory construction. When using rational choice theory to investigate a particular social or political phenomenon, one is buying into the theoretical premise that either people are rational in their actions or they act as if they are rational. This is different from a more stimulus-response approach to human behavior that argues that this behavior is much the product of social milieu and environmental influences. Thus, the contrast between a rational choice perspective and a stimulus-response perspective can be seen in some respects as one of theoretical polar opposites.

Systems theory, and thus graph algebra, does not require a theoretical assumption of rationality. Similarly, systems theory does not require that the theorist embed a stimulus-response perspective into a theory, nor does systems theory deny that possibility. But what systems theory does demand is that the system itself be considered as an entire entity, and this, in essence, is the only invariant "theory" of systems theory. Systems theory demands that the components of the system do not and cannot fully explain the phenomenon under investigation outside of the system. This is the most crucial conceptual characteristic of systems theory, and one usually adopts this conceptual characteristic when one uses graph algebra. I say "usually" because it is possible, of course, to use graph algebra in a systems-neutral fashion, as is done in Figure 2.2, which is a graph algebra representation of a linear regression model. But once one develops nearly any model that is more complex than that, one starts thinking of the system as an entire entity that cannot still be understood if one takes the components out of the model and looks at them independently of one another.

To develop a systems theory model using graph algebra, one first collects the inputs and the outputs and then specifies the possible transformations with whatever complexity is required. After the model is constructed, analysis of the model begins. One of the great strengths of the systems approach is that a researcher is not limited to an analysis of the model as it applies to only an existing body of data. Counterfactual analysis can also be performed. This is essentially a "what if" game in which researchers use simulations of the model under hypothetical situations as a means of investigating the overall nature of the system itself. Thus, one can better understand a system if one extends its actual operation over a wider range of possibilities than the one for which historical data exist. This enhances the ability of a researcher to use the model predictively for a variety of scenarios. For example, with respect to destruction of the Earth's environment, we will want to know what the possibilities are for the future precisely so that we may attempt to avoid the more dire situations. Simulating a systems model under a variety of potential conditions of, say, global warming, allows us to do this.

Systems analysis also allows researchers to test for underlying character-istics of the model given an existing body of data as well. This is not the counterfactual case, but rather the exploratory prodding of a systems model to force it to reveal hidden response mechanisms that help explain why the past occurred in the manner recorded by history. The examination of a system's memory through the investigation of its half-life (a subject common to nearly all introductory differential and difference equation texts) is one example of this type of analysis.

Systems and Equilibria

The concept of equilibrium is crucial to understanding the theoretical content of the systems approach. There are three types of equilibria at issue. The first we will call "the equilibrium of system stability." A system can operate such that it is in a state of balance, so that inputs are transformed into outputs and the system's essential characteristics are maintained for some specified time. Thus, we can say that a system of government is in a state of equilibrium as long as it is able to perpetuate itself. When, say, a system of democratic government falls apart due to a military takeover, we can say that the democratic system has ended and a new system of military dictatorship has begun. This is an example of diachronic change. But as long as one system continues to operate, we can say that the system itself is in equilibrium.

The second type of equilibrium relevant to systems we will call "the equilibrium of variable stability." This equilibrium relates to the values of the output. That is, when a system is defined through an appropriate collection of inputs, outputs, and rules of transformation, then that system can be described in terms of an algebraic structure, which, indeed, is the primary topic of this book. That algebraic structure is then wedded to variable and parameter values. In many cases, the correct combination of variable and parameter values can lead to an outcome that remains in a constant steady state, a periodic limit cycle, or, in more complex systems, a stable state of bounded chaotic variation defined in terms of a strange attractor. Thus, we can say that the system has achieved a state of dynamic equilibrium. This implies that the trajectories of the system's phase space have been captured in the basin of an equilibrium attractor and have arrived at or near this equilibrium, however this equilibrium may be defined.

It is important to note that systems operate in time, but their structures usually (see below) do not depend on time. In this respect, it is said that systems themselves are time invariant when modeling synchronic change. This means that the structure of any given system remains constant for a given duration. Systems operate to transform inputs into outputs not because the inputs are associated with any given time, but because the inputs have the values that they have. The same inputs can reoccur at different times and the system will transform those later inputs identically as it transformed the earlier inputs. The values of the inputs and outputs thus may vary within any given system's structure as long as the system's structure itself remains constant. Indeed, this is implied by the equilibrium of system stability as discussed above (see also Cortés et al., 1974, pp. 278–279).

Why must we say that systems are "usually" time invariant rather than absolutely time invariant? In legacy discussions of systems theory, it was typical to think of systems in terms of constant structures that operate on variables. But both mathematical and systems theory advances are now blurring this previously absolute characterization of system structure as time invariant. For example, catastrophe theory now allows for the description of systems that experience radical and sudden transformations in variable values, something that can also be accomplished with graph algebra using conditional paths. Thus, while system continuity used to imply incremental (i.e., proportional) change among the state variables, this restriction no longer applies for some cleverly constructed systems. What formerly would have required the abandonment of one system and the creation of a new system can now sometimes be resolved within the boundaries of a single more sophisticated system, often of highly nonlinear characterization. Thus, whether or not a system is time invariant is sometimes dependent on our ability to describe a social phenomenon parsimoniously using one time invariant theory. When that fails, we may need to employ two or more different systems. Then we face the question of whether or not the separate systems can be linked.

This brings us to the third category of equilibrium that is relevant to the current discussion, which we will call "meta-equilibrium." Meta-equilibrium occurs when a sequence of systems emerge, one system from the other, all linked in a definable manner. As one system becomes obsolete due to, say, evolutionary changes in the system's external environment, then that system collapses and a new system emerges. This new system similarly follows a process of growth, maintenance, decay, and eventual collapse. From this demise arises a new system, and the cycle continues. This produces what is called a "system cascade," and one can argue that system cascades are the norm for everything in nature. The meta-equilibrium characterizes the fixed structure of the system cascade. Thus, we have a "metasystem," which is the collection of all systems that produce a sequentially evolving system cascade, and that metasystem has its own stable structure, which we can say is in a stable state of meta-equilibrium. Talking about systems as component parts of larger systems is a standard ingredient of systems theory, and this is necessary to describe many large-scale social and political phenomena. (For an alternate perspective of this issue, see Cortés et al., 1974, pp. 289–291.)

Let us consider all of this from the perspective of some elemental social theory, beginning with suggestions made by Robert A. Nisbet (1969). I offer this not as a definitive statement, but as one possible way of looking at the idea of a meta-equilibrium within the context of metasystems. Nisbet has argued forcefully that social change is inevitable and cannot be avoided altogether under any circumstance. There is no dichotomy between stability and change, for change is constant. Thus, the idea of anything remaining the same must be abandoned, and this includes the structure of any given system. At first this seems to contradict our previous discussion relating to a system's constancy with respect to time, but a deeper look forces this contradiction to disappear. From Nisbet's perspective, all systems evolve from lower levels of order to higher levels of order. To some extent, we can expect the higher levels of order to be more complex than the lower levels, but added complexity is not a requirement. What is required is the understanding that lower-level systems give rise to the higher-level systems. Thus, with all systems, we have an evolution from one system to another, with each new system containing within it the seed of the subsequent system that will take the place of the former. Thus, the change from one system to another is directional. Formerly we have thought of change within one system as being directional, in the sense that the fixed system structure transforms inputs into outputs according to rules that determine a sense of direction. But now we can speak of sequential change of structure across systems as being directional as well.

From Nisbet's perspective, change is continuous. This is a result of the natural evolution in the potential for change in system structure. Thus, it may seem that a particular system is time invariant for a period of time, but this apparently fixed structure is merely a relative constancy of dominant processes. At any given moment within any system, changes occur that will ultimately force a structural change in the dominant system linkages that define that system's structure. That these changes remain so small that they are essentially unnoticed from the perspective of the continued operation of the dominant system linkages should not worry us. We study systems precisely because the potential for future structural change remains visibly dormant for extended periods of time, thereby allowing us to examine the functioning of the dominant system linkages in the temporary absence of structural change.

Consider these ideas in the context of Rostow's view of economic development (Rostow, 1960). Essentially, Rostow conceived of long-term economic development as a process spanning six distinct stages. Each stage can be considered as one distinct system. The first stage is traditional society, which is agriculturally based. This stage is followed by structural changes in the forms of information that are available to traditional societies.

These structural changes are due to both indigenous technological advances as well as advances resultant from contact with more advanced societies. This second stage is followed by a third period of rapid industrial growth combined with the emergence of mechanized and commercial agriculture. Subsequent to this is the emergence of a wealthy society. This leads to a system dominated by consumerism and mass consumption. Finally, consumerism and mass consumption yield to a society that seeks advances in the quality of life, or what Inglehart and others might call the age of postmaterialism. Each of these stages constitutes an identifiable system, each of which can be described separately. Yet the entire sequence of systems is also a system, a metasystem.

There is, of course, a political analog to Rostow's economic ideas, and perhaps the most relevant to the current discussion is that proposed by Organski (1965). Organski envisioned four primary stages of political development, each one of which can be considered as a distinct system. The first stage is primitive unification, and this is where a national government is initially established, and its primary purpose is to consolidate its basic functioning. For example, this stage corresponds with the emergence of independent nations in, say, Africa following the period of colonization. Following the period of governmental consolidation, the purpose of government changes to one of promoting national economic growth, and this often implies governmental encouragement toward industrialization. The third stage results from the fact that industrialization is always accompanied by social and economic hardship on the part of large segments of the masses. People move from rural areas to urban areas in search of jobs, and companies are rarely stable employers for many of these new workers in competitive economic environments that require constant reevaluation of production processes. Governments are required to cushion these transitional hardships lest the populace express their discontent to the point of threatening the long-term stability of the state. Finally, a period of abundance arrives, and the government's primary responsibility is one of assisting in the transition to a largely automated economy.

This then raises the question of how one addresses the issue of system change. If systems carry within them the potential for change, and this potential is constantly evolving to the point where it eventually manifests itself as diachronic change, how do we model this? Some theorists will want to limit their investigations of social systems to distinct periods of structural constancy, essentially ignoring variations in potential for structural change. Nearly always these changes in potential are a consequence of evolutionary changes in the environments within which systems are embedded. Yet one can only ignore those environmental changes for so long before they eventually emerge with sufficient power to destroy the old system and establish a new one. But other theorists will want to extend their discussions of systems to include the transitions between systems. Any such treatment is a discussion of a metasystem.

To address metasystems, one must focus on the crises that manifest at the end of one system and the emergence of another. Rarely does a system collapse without the appearance of some noticeable crisis. For example, in parallel to Organski's ideas of political development, Lucian Pye has proposed a set of accompanying crises that bridge the gap between the sequential stages of development (Pye, 1971). The first is the identity crisis, and this is where the government establishes the idea among its citizens that they indeed are members of this new nation. For example, after the colonization period in East Africa, the primary responsibility of the national leaders was to instill into the sensibilities of the new citizens that they were Tanzanians, Kenyans, or Ugandans. Different leaders accomplished this differently. In Tanzania, Julius Nyerere essentially sealed his nation's borders and followed a policy of *Ujamaa*, or forced collectivization of agriculture, combined with the required national use of the Swahili language. The second of Pye's crises is the legitimacy crisis. At first, the nation largely agrees on the scope of the government's responsibilities. Eventually, there is a participation crisis as social and political groups both form and mature and then begin to demand more of the political system. The state then responds to these demands by building bureaucratic infrastructure in what Pye calls the penetration crisis. Finally, there is the distribution crisis in which the state becomes responsible for allocating various natural and economic resources.

Thus, when systems collapse, the societies pass through crises, and these crises are the hours of birth for the new systems that emerge from that which existed previously. From this perspective, no single system is truly separate from the system that follows it or from the system that precedes it. Minimally, the end of one system constitutes the initial condition for the subsequent system. Crucially, if one is to model a metasystem, then one might incorporate the crises of system transition as one of the outputs of the metasystem. Giving examples of this extends beyond the scope of this book, but it nonetheless is possible to do with the graph algebra described here. It may be necessary in some cases to measure these crisis outputs as probabilities rather than as singular events, in the manner of event history analysis (alternatively, hazard analysis, survival analysis, etc.) or even logistic regression. A useful introductory treatment of how to proceed using probabilistic differential equations that give rise to entire events can be found in May (1974, pp. 26–36).

The above discussion of system cascades has a flip side. While I have discussed the potential for the longitudinal evolution of a system's structure, I have not addressed the potential for interaction between horizontally placed systems. For example, if there is a system in one geographical area at a certain point in time, this system may influence a different system in another geographical area. Of course, it is possible that geographically separated systems may be mutually exclusive, and the possibility of system exclusiveness suggests potential boundaries on our investigations of any one system. This is a useful point to make when considering the practical feasibility of any single study of human behavior. For any given system, one can always find examples of other systems with which there is no interaction. Using an extreme example, the tribal squabbles of indigenous groups living in the Amazon jungle hardly influence the probability of an arms race between North Korea and South Korea.

To summarize, in this book I have explained and extended the language of graph algebra that was originally developed by Cortés et al. (1974). I have also updated its application with respect to new mathematical and social-theoretical concerns. Using this language, scholars can describe social systems in algebraic form. The great strength of this language is that it uses schematic representations that both enable and encourage sophisticated algebraic specifications of these systems. As a language, and as with any language, graph algebra is technically neutral with respect to social theory. But the language of graph algebra is based on the idea that systems exist, and the language is specifically designed to assist in the description of the structure of these systems. Thus, when we use graph algebra, we buy into the idea that systems are real entities worthy of description. When we say that a system is fixed, we refer to its apparent stability over a period of time. This does not ignore the fact that each system carries within itself the seed of its own destruction. It only says that we can analyze any system for as long as it exists.

All modelers make compromises in deciding what to include in a model of any given social or political phenomenon. Thus, as modelers we admit to the fact that all our models are incomplete. Indeed, their incompleteness is one of the great advantages of good models. The best models are those that capture only that which is most essential to describe the dominant characteristics of any phenomenon. We avoid completeness by seeking parsimony, and there is always that trade-off with modeling. Graph algebra assists us in making the most of parsimony. Beyond merely extending the list of independent variables for a multiple regression, we can increase our model's explanatory power by using graph algebra to portray a greater level of structural complexity with respect to the relationships among the variables that we already employ. As such, graph algebra is a language that helps us raise the potential content and sophistication of our theories. The theories are not products of the language. They are products of our own thinking, and their value is limited only by our ingenuity in determining the causal mechanisms that underlie the scientific problems before us.

REFERENCES

Aczel, A. D. (2003). *Entanglement: The unlikely story of how scientists, mathematicians, and philosophers proved Einstein's spookiest theory*. New York: Plume.

Allen, R. G. D. (1963). *Mathematical economics* (2nd ed.). New York: St. Martin's Press.

Ashby, W. R. (1956). *An introduction to cybernetics*. London: Chapman & Hall.

Baumol, W. J. (1970). *Economic dynamics: An introduction*. New York: Macmillan.

von Bertalanffy, L. (1976). *General system theory: Foundations, development, applications*. New York: George Braziller.

Blanchard, P., Devaney, R. L., & Hall, G. R. (2006). *Differential equations* (3rd ed.). Belmont, CA: Thomson—Brooks/Cole.

Brown, C. (1991). *Ballots of tumult: A portrait of volatility in American voting*. Ann Arbor: University of Michigan Press.

Brown, C. (1995a). *Serpents in the sand: Essays on the nonlinear nature of politics and human destiny*. Ann Arbor: University of Michigan Press.

Brown, C. (1995b). *Chaos and catastrophe theories*. Thousand Oaks, CA: Sage.

Brown, C. (2007). *Differential equations: A modeling approach*. Thousand Oaks, CA: Sage.

Brown, C. (2008). Nonlinear dynamics, chaos, and catastrophe theory. In S. Menard (Ed.), *The handbook of longitudinal research*. San Diego, CA: Elsevier.

Cohen, B. P. (1980). The conditional nature of scientific knowledge. In L. Freeze (Ed.), *Theoretical methods in sociology: Seven essays* (pp. 71–110). Pittsburgh, PA: University of Pittsburgh Press.

Cohen, B. P. (1989). *Developing sociological knowledge: Theory and method* (2nd ed.). Chicago: Nelson Hall.

Cortés, F., Przeworski, A., & Sprague, J. (1974). *Systems analysis for social scientists*. New York: Wiley.

Danby, J. M. A. (1997). *Computer modeling: From sports to spaceflight . . . From order to chaos*. Richmond, VA: Willmann-Bell.

Duvall, R. D., & Freeman, J. R. (1983). The techno-bureaucratic elite and the entrepreneurial state in dependent industrialization. *American Political Science Review, 77*(3), 569–587.

The Empirical Implications of Theoretical Models. (2002). Report of the Political Science Program, Directorate for Social, Behavioral and Economic Sciences, National Science Foundation. Retrieved from http://www.nsf.gov/sbe/ses/polisci/reports/pdf/eitmreport.pdf.

Filkins, D. (2005, January 26). Conflict in Iraq: Campaign; Insurgents vowing to kill Iraqis who brave the polls on Sunday. *The New York Times*, p. A1[N].

Goldberg, S. (1958). *Introduction to difference equations*. New York: Wiley.

Goldstein, L. J., Schneider, D. I., & Siegel, M. J. (1988). *Finite mathematics and its applications* (3rd ed.). Englewood Cliffs, NJ: Prentice-Hall.

Gottman, J. M., Murray, J. D., Swanson, C., Tyson, R., & Swanson, K. R. (2003). *The mathematics of marriage: Dynamic nonlinear models*. Cambridge: MIT Press.

Haberman, R. (1977). *Mathematical models: Mechanical vibrations, population dynamics, and traffic flow*. Englewood Cliffs, NJ: Prentice-Hall.

Hamming, R. (1971). *Introduction to applied numerical analysis*. New York: McGraw-Hill.

Hamming, R. (1973). *Numerical methods for scientists and engineers* (2nd ed.). New York: McGraw-Hill.

Huckfeldt, R. R., Kohfeld, C. W., & Likens, T. W. (1982). *Dynamic modeling: An introduction*. Newbury Park, CA: Sage.

Kiel, L. D., & Elliott, E. (1996). *Chaos theory in the social sciences: Foundations and applications*. Ann Arbor: University of Michigan Press.

Liao, T. F. (1990). A unified three-dimensional framework of theory construction and development in sociology. *Sociological Theory, 8*(1), 85–98.

Liao, T. F. (1992). Theory construction and development in sociology: A reply to Willer and to Harris and Walker. *Sociological Theory, 10*(1), 118–121.

Lorenz, E. N. (1963). Deterministic non-periodic flow. *Journal of Atmospheric Science, 20,* 130–141.

Ludwig, D., Jones, D. S., & Holling, C. S. (1978). Qualitative analysis of insect outbreak systems: The spruce budworm and the forest. *Journal of Animal Ecology, 47,* 315–332.

Mare, R. D., & Winship, C. (1984). The paradox of lessening racial inequality and joblessness among black youth: Enrollment, enlistment, and employment, 1964–1981. *American Sociological Review, 49*(1), 39–55.

May, R. M. (1974). *Stability and complexity in model ecosystems* (2nd ed.). Princeton, NJ: Princeton University Press.

Miller, J. G. (1978). *Living systems.* New York: McGraw-Hill.

Nisbet, R. A. (1969). *Social change and history.* New York: Oxford University Press.

Organski, A. F. K. (1965). *Stages of political development.* New York: Knopf.

Ostrom, C. W. (1990). *Time series analysis* (2nd ed.). Thousand Oaks, CA: Sage.

Przeworski, A. (1975). Institutionalization of voting patterns, or is mobilization the source of decay. *American Political Science Review, 69,* 49–67.

Przeworski, A., & Sprague, J. (1986). *Paper stones: A history of electoral socialism.* Chicago: University of Chicago Press.

Pye, L. W. (1971). Foreword. In L. Binder, J. S. Coleman, J. LaPalombara, L. W. Pye, S. Verba, & M. Weiner (Eds.), *Crises and sequences in political development* (p. vii). Princeton, NJ: Princeton University Press.

Richards, D. (Ed.). (2000). *Political complexity: Nonlinear models of politics.* Ann Arbor: University of Michigan Press.

Richardson, L. F. (1960). *Arms and insecurity.* Chicago: Quadrangle Books.

Rostow, W. W. (1960). *Stages of economic growth: A non-communist manifesto.* Cambridge, UK: Cambridge University Press.

Signorino, C. S., & Yilmaz, K. (2003). Strategic misspecification in regression models. *American Journal of Political Science, 47*(3), 551–566.

Toulmin, S. (1953). *The philosophy of science.* London: Hutchinson.

Walker, H. A., & Cohen, B. P. (1985). Scope statements: Imperatives for evaluating theory. *American Sociological Review, 50*(3), 288–301.

Weinberg, G. M. (1975). *An introduction to general systems thinking.* New York: Dorset House.

Yardley, J. (2005, January 31). Fearing future, China starts to give girls their due. *The New York Times,* p. A3[N].

Zill, D. G. (2005). *A first course in differential equations with modeling applications* (8th ed.). Belmont, CA: Thomson—Brooks/Cole.

INDEX

94

ABOUT THE AUTHOR

Courtney Brown began his teaching career as a college calculus instructor in Africa before moving on to teach nonlinear differential and difference equation modeling in the social sciences at the University of California at Los Angeles, Emory University, and the Interuniversity Consortium for Political and Social Research Summer Program at the University of Michigan. He has published numerous books on applied nonlinear mathematical modeling in the social sciences, including *Serpents in the Sand: Essays on the Nonlinear Nature of Politics and Human Destiny, Ballots of Tumult: A Portrait of Volatility in American Voting, Chaos and Catastrophe Theories,* and *Differential Equations: A Modeling Approach.* Also of scholarly interest, although independent of his mathematical and social science work as a college professor, he has published a science book on the subject of nonlocal consciousness and physics, *Remote Viewing: The Science and Theory of Nonphysical Perception,* an area of research that has gained attention in select physics and psychology circles. He received his Ph.D. degree from Washington University, St. Louis, in 1981 in political science with an emphasis on mathematical modeling.

Rarely has a new approach to theory development of [...] affecting the way social scientists develop mathemat[...] political phenomena as graph algebra. **Graph Algebr[...] With a Systems Approach** by Courtney Brown introduces this new modeling tool to students and researchers in the social sciences. Derived from engineering literature that uses similar techniques to map electronic circuits and physical systems, graph algebra uses a systems approach to modeling that offers social scientists a variety of tools that are both sophisticated and easily applied.

Key Features

- *Incorporates social theory:* An easily applied language of mathematical modeling is used to algebraically "flesh out" even the most complicated and sophisticated theories.

- *Uses social science examples of graph algebra models:* Many examples illustrate how graph algebra can be used to model theories from a wide variety of substantive areas and disciplines.

- *Explains linear and nonlinear model specifications using graph algebra from a social science perspective:* Readers can move beyond simple linear regression models by using graph algebra.

- *Assists readers in developing their own difference and differential equation model specifications:* Graph algebra can be used with difference equations as easily as differential equations, allowing readers to work with models in both discrete and continuous time.

- *Makes the specification of social systems easy:* Social systems are modeled using multiple-equation, interdependent systems of equations.

- *Offers great flexibility in model specification:* Graph algebra can be used to model social systems in which certain relationships operate under conditional paths and scope conditions.

Intended Audience

Designed for readers in the social sciences with minimal mathematical training, this text is ideal for advanced undergraduate and graduate courses such as Statis[...] Modeling, Quantitative Methods, and Applied Mathematics in a variety of disc[...] including statistics, political science, sociology, economics, and psychology.

ISBN 978-1-4129-4109-9

Visit our Web site at www.sagepublications.com

 **SAGE** Publications

Los Angeles • London • New Delhi • Singapore